Prisoner of War Ship Models
1775–1825

0 1 2 3 4 5 6 7 Inches

Prisoner of War Ship Models
1775–1825

Ewart C. Freeston

CONWAY
MARITIME PRESS

© EWART C FREESTON, 1973

All rights reserved. Unauthorised
duplication contravenes applicable laws.

First published in Great Britain by
Nautical Publishing Company Ltd,
Lymington.

Reprinted 1987 by
CONWAY MARITIME PRESS LTD
24 Bride Lane, Fleet Street
London EC4Y 8DR

ISBN 0 8517 7 468 7

Printed by The Camelot Press Ltd,
London and Southampton
Bound by Butler & Tanner Ltd, Frome

Frontispiece A charming Prisoner-of-War bone ship model only nine and a half inches overall (a little larger than this photograph). Though purporting to be a model of the GLORY 98 guns, it cannot be said (as with so many others having famous names inscribed on them) to be a true representation of this vessel; but as an unusually colourful example of a bone model it is possibly unique. The engraved and painted base immediately catches the eye, though there are many other points of interest, as for instance the deck fittings, capstans, boats, deck house and anchor; and the carved and painted figurehead of an armed warrior in a cloak. The rigging also is good with cable laid shrouds and stays set up with lanyards to dead-eyes or hearts, and the rigging leading through tiny bone blocks. Said to have been made at Chatham, this is a most attractive specimen. *Courtesy of The Parker Gallery and The Connoisseur*

To my wife
EDNA
without whose help and encouragement
this book could not have been written

Contents

An impressive bow view of LE VENGEUR, a French 74 gun ship. This bone model was made by prisoners in Portchester Castle in 1798 and well illustrates the high quality and careful attention to detail of some of the best examples. The Science Museum, London

List of Illustrations

Illustrations (*continued*)

Acknowledgements

This book is the result of months of careful research. It has entailed the visiting of many museums, the interviewing of many people, the writing of many letters and the travelling of many miles. Consequently I am indebted in no small way to a great number of persons, to name all of whom would be impossible and serve no useful purpose. However, I would like to acknowledge with sincere thanks the help received from the following sources in the assembly of this material:

Miss Vera D. Freeston
Mr. W. H. Honey
Mr. A. Ebelthite
Mr. Arthur R. Sawers
The Science Museum
The National Maritime Museum
Trinity House Museum
Peterborough Museum
The Museum and Art Gallery, Luton
The United States Naval Academy
    Museum

The Parker Gallery
Arlington Court Museum
The City of Liverpool Museum
Musée d'Art et d'Histoire, Geneva
The University of Liverpool
Le Musée de la Marine, Paris
Christie, Manson & Woods Ltd.
The Museum of Fine Arts, Boston
Sotheby & Co. Ltd.
The Glasgow Museum and Art
    Gallery

To these and many others who have provided me with information, suggested lines of enquiry or given me clues to follow in my research, my thanks are due.

Herstmonceux, 1973   *Ewart C. Freeston*

Prologue

It is a curious fact that many of the greatest works of art have been created in places and under conditions which, one would think, would have militated against any success in the production of a masterpiece. This applies to all forms of art whether it be literature, painting, music or, in the case of the subject under review, the making of model ships and boats. Though the accomplished craftsman can work with tools and equipment which would spell failure to the unskilled amateur, yet even so it would seem to be necessary for the skilled workman to possess the best tools and work under the best conditions in order to create something of beauty. For though the expert is master of his tools and trade, and can produce with inferior equipment a result which the novice would find impossible with the very best, there would seem to be a minimum necessary for even ordinary productions. So granting this premise the results we see achieved in the subject now being discussed can fill us only with wonder and amazement at the skill, patience, ingenuity and fortitude displayed by these unknown, but now I hope not unsung, seamen of an era long since past, who did their work under the most distasteful, sordid and terrible conditions of body and mind, with tools and equipment of a most primitive sort.

Chapter 1

The Prisoner-of-War Ship Models which are the subject of this book were made in an age of revolution in political, intellectual and industrial spheres. A new concept of war was taking place, the rights of the individual were being recognized and the machine was about to lighten the labour of the worker. But though this is neither a historical survey nor a historical treatise, it is an advantage to know what were the principal events of the time as they affected this country and the rest of the world.

King George III was on the throne of Great Britain and was succeeded in 1820 by his son King George IV who since 1811, on account of the insanity of his father, had been Prince Regent. The war with America had recently ended and her Independence recognized by Great Britain in 1783, though this did not bring the complete easing of friction between the two countries, as will be seen in the later references to American prisoners. In France it was Louis XVI who was king, to be followed a few years after his execution by Napoleon Buonaparte as the leader of the destinies of the nation.

It was in 1793 that France declared war on England and Holland, and from February of that year until 1815, interupted for a brief interval in 1802 by the Peace of Amiens (which was scarcely more than an uneasy truce), the British nation was engaged in hostilities not only with the French but also with many other European nations, and even at one time finding herself the sole opposing force to that of Napoleon and his accumulated military and naval might, the greatest and most powerful the Continent had seen until that time.

But though on land Napoleon's successes had been spectacular, progressive and seemingly unpreventable, on the sea it was a very different story. In fact it was his failure here that obstructed the fulfilment of his dream of European, if not world, domination. For as Captain Mahan commented, "What stood between 'La Grande Armée' and the dominion of the world were the English battleships on which they never looked."

The victory of Nelson at Trafalgar on 21 October 1805 put an end to Napoleon's threat of invasion, while the victory of Wellington at Waterloo on 18 June 1815 spelt the final eclipse of Napoleon as a European menace.

This, very briefly, was the international situation for the period with which we are concerned and during the whole of this time, between about 1775 and 1815, when untold thousands of many nations perished in the holocaust, huge numbers of prisoners were taken; for it is estimated that even during the years between 1803 and 1814 alone, no less than 122,440 captured soldiers and sailors were brought to this country, with a maximum in 1814 of 72,000. On the cessation of hostilities the repatriation of the tens of thousands of prisoners then began, bringing to these sufferers of man's inhumanity, some of whom had been in captivity for upwards of twelve years, the sight of their homes and loved ones they had not seen for perhaps twenty years.

The prisons of the late eighteenth and early nineteenth centuries were morally degrading and utterly insanitary places, and no humane consideration was allowed to interfere with the course of justice and if a man were condemned to imprisonment, then the building in which he would find himself would be a fearsome and terrrible place, for the idea of using prisons as places of reform had as yet not developed.

Prisoners were incarcerated either in gaols, the supervision of which was the responsibility of the justices and the local authorities, and were a charge on the parish; or else, at the time of which we are speaking, in prison ships moored in several estuaries round the southern coasts. These latter were also used by the prison authorities as reception centres for those awaiting transportation to Australia or the West Indies, amongst other places, and thus came under the jurisdiction of that section of the government known as the Transport Office.

The lot of the prisoners of war was not greatly different from that of the civil prisoners, except in so far as they were subject to the internationally agreed treatment of men taken in battle by a successful opponent. Therefore we find that the men taken prisoner, either on sea or land, were disposed of in one of the three following ways:

A. By confinement in prison ships afloat.
B. By confinement in buildings ashore.
C. By release on parole.

These three ways of keeping the prisoners of war must be considered in some detail if a better understanding of the conditions under which they passed their time, the difficulties, the ennui and the misery they endured, and the methods by which they overcame their troubles, is to be appreciated.

The hulks First then, the prison ships: these were either disused or condemned ships for which the Navy had no further use, or else captured enemy vessels too badly damaged to be economically refitted so as to be of further service to the fighting forces. They were moored in certain rivers and harbours round the coast, notably, amongst others, at Chatham, Portsmouth, Plymouth and Gillingham Creek. They were termed the hulks; a word which by its very sound describes the repulsive and hateful objects they had been made. For there is little doubt that the great majority of them were veritably floating hells, a view supported whenever reference is made to them. In appearance they had been transformed from structures of beauty (for the wooden walls of the 1800's had a majestic beauty of their own, even if we might consider them now heavy and unwieldy vessels) to monsters of ugliness. They had been stripped of masts, sails and rigging, their carved and gilded embellishments removed and their chequerboard topsides smudged out with tar to an unhealthy looking and repulsive black. The hull sides had been built up and accommodation provided, in the form of deck houses for the officers and guards.

All the guns and heavy equipment had also been removed from the interior of the vessel which in consequence drew less water, so bringing the orlop deck—that is, the lowest deck of all and usually below—above the level of the water. Narrow scuttles had been cut in the hull sides to admit light to this deck and these and the existing gun ports were filled with cast iron grilles with bars two inches thick which defied any attempt on the part of the prisoners to escape by filing through them.

3

The lieutenant in charge and other officers were quartered aft, and about fifty soldiers forward, with heavy iron-studded timber bulkheads separating them from the prisoners who were confined on the decks amidships. The bulkheads were pierced at intervals by spy holes both for observation and, if the necessity arose, for quelling a riot with the use of firearms in safety by the guards.

Just above the water line, all round the ship was built a gallery with an open slatted floor to prevent an escaping prisoner from hiding

PRISON-SHIP. IN PORTSMOUTH HARBOUR.
CONVICTS going on board.

1.1 This drawing by E. W. Cooke, 1828, shows convicts going on board H.M.S. YORK when she was moored as a prison hulk in Portsmouth Harbour.

The YORK was built in 1807 as a 74 gun third-rate but she did not become a prison ship until 1819, right at the end of the period under discussion here. However, she is typical of other prison ships and hulks moored in various estuaries during this era. (See Appendix II)

beneath it unseen by the sentries who paced along it both day and night, the monotony broken only by the repetition at regular intervals of a quarter of an hour of the cry of "All's well".

Inside the ship where the prisoners were confined, all superfluous fittings had been removed from the decks and replaced with only a bench running along the inside of the hull and by a few more placed athwartships. Here the prisoners lived a crowded and communal existence, the state of which we can gain some idea when we read that if four hundred civil convicts were kept on a hulk, the numbers of prisoners of war ranged between eight hundred and a thousand on one of equivalent size. For a specific example we have the fact that in 1813 in the BRUNSWICK at Chatham, no less than 460 men slept on the orlop deck, a space of only 125 feet long, 40 feet at the widest part and about 4 feet 10 inches in height; circumstances to which one can only compare the proverbial sardine!

At night all the port holes were closed to be reopened at six o'clock in the morning in the summer or at eight o'clock in the winter. Then the foetid air belched out with such an overpowering odour that the guard detailed for the duty invariably jumped back to avoid the foul air! In exceptionally hot weather the port holes were sometimes left open, otherwise many of the prisoners must inevitably have died of suffocation; and so the living conditions aboard the hulks can be easily imagined. The men slept in hammocks slung side by side from the deck pillars or, if insufficient space were available, in tiers as well. For the prisoners with money a kind of swinging cradle was obtainable, which may have been slightly more comfortable but did not alter the oppressive stench and the vermin.

These conditions, allied with poor food, inferior in quality, and the heartlessness of the officers, combined with the repeated examples of cruelty must have made the hulks ghastly and terrifying places. De Moras, the French administrator, writing in reference to complaints of cruelty, says, "... *des Français prisonniers pour la faute la plus légère ... et que celui est chargé de fers, mis en cachot et perd toute espérance de liberté.*" Some of those in authority undoubtedly did attempt to make the lot of the prisoner as bearable as possible, though it must be admitted with reluctance that these were deplorably few, for the opportunity and likelihood of "pickings" were ever present and easy to achieve by substituting inferior and smaller issues of food with the help and connivance of the contractors; as one French writer says on this point, "... *du biscuit aussy mal* ...

le viande ne vaut pas mieux. Je ne l'attribue qu'à l'infidélité et l'avidité des entrepreneurs."

1
As recorded by *Chambers's Journal*, 1854, no. 21, page 330

It is as well to realize, however, that the hulks were used originally as prisons for civil offenders and later on as places of confinement for the malefactors and recalcitrant amongst the prisoners.[1] But in spite of this, there is little doubt they were insanitary, inconvenient and above all uneconomical, since for a 74 gun ship in which were 700 prisoners, the upkeep amounted to £5869 annually; whereas the annual expense at Dartmoor prison for 6000 prisoners was only £2862, the equivalent of eight hulked 74's at a cost of no less than £46,952.

Eventually it was realized that with the enormous number of prisoners being brought to this country, some other means of providing for them must be found, for the hulks were becoming inadequate for the accommodation of the new arrivals. This brings us to the second

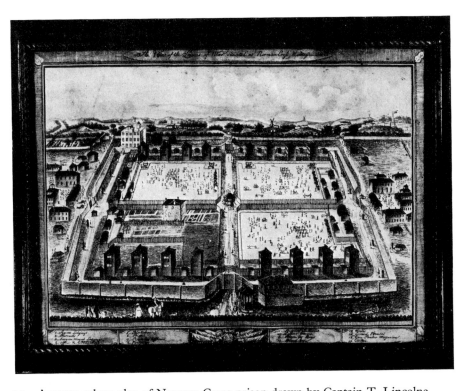

1.2   A water colour plan of Norman Cross prison drawn by Captain T. Lincolne Barker, Governor of Norman Cross barracks, 1810. The view shown is looking south. The modern Norman Cross Memorial is situated just outside the prison on the right or western side at the present crossroads on the Great North Road. Stilton Church can be seen at the extreme right background of this water colour. *Peterborough Museum and Maxwell Art Gallery*

method of housing the prisoners, that of confinement in prisons ashore. At first they were lodged in borough gaols such as the Savoy and Wellclose Square in London; strong houses such as the Wool House in Southampton; country houses as at Sissinghurst in Kent; adapted farms as at Roscrow and Kergilliack in Cornwall. In barracks at Winchester, Edinburgh, Portchester Castle, Forton near Gosport, Hillsea near Portsmouth and also in prisons at Bristol, Plymouth, Liverpool, Manchester, Dorchester and many other places.[2]

Then in 1796 the first prison was built specially for prisoners of war. This was at Norman Cross, and was intended to hold a maximum of 7000 men, the first of whom entered the prison on 7 April 1797. After this, in 1806 the prison on Dartmoor was built for about 6000 men. Intended to be only a temporary building, it has lasted to the present day in accordance with the saying that in England nothing is so permanent as the temporary. The gates of the prison opened on 24 May 1809 and it became in 1850 the convict prison of which we all know. The third of the prisons was that at Perth and was opened on 6 August 1812, which became in 1839 the general prison. All these places were officially known as Depots, and were always referred to as such by the authorities.

Norman Cross prison, five or six miles from Peterborough, was built of wood. The various sections were prefabricated in London and erected on the site. This was of about forty acres on the high ground which is to the north of the road to Peterborough, at the junction with the Great North Road. No remains of the prison itself are now to be seen on account of its structure; and when its purpose was fulfilled, was dismantled and sold piecemeal by auction. The only remaining buildings on the site are three brick-built houses used as private residences which at the time of building were the Barrack Master's house, the Superintendent's house and the Agent's house, all bordering the Peterborough road.

To the traveller speeding along the highway there is one other visible sign of its existence, if he cares to stop and read the inscription: it is a memorial column of stone at the top of which is a bronze winged eagle. It was erected opposite the site on the Great North Road in 1914 in remembrance of the 1770 prisoners who died in the prison during the time it was occupied from 1797 to 1814 and who were buried in the low-lying field which slopes away from the road.

2
See Appendix II

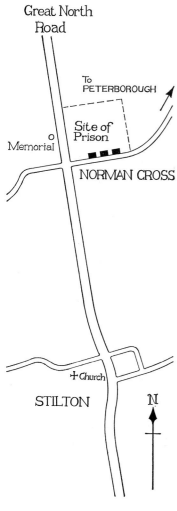

1.3 Sketch map of the situation of Norman Cross prison. Not to scale. Stilton is now by-passed by the new Great North Road

The prison was roughly octagonal in shape, crossed from side to side by two paths, at the intersection of which stood the Block House armed with guns, the guards commanding the four quadrangles so formed. In each of these quadrangles (sarcastically called the *prés* by the prisoners) stood four caserns which constituted the prisons for about 500 men each. Surrounding the prison grounds was at first a high stockade fence through which, said Mr. Lewin of Yaxley in 1890, the prisoners at the time of his boyhood hung out bags crying to the travellers and pedestrians on the road, "Drop a penny in my bag". There was a model of the prison in the Musée de l'Armée at Les Invalides in Paris, but which, I am informed, has now unaccountably disappeared. It was made by one of the prisoners, by name M. Foulley, and a photograph of the model may be seen in T. J. Walker's book, *The Depot for Prisoners of War at Norman Cross*.

1.4 Memorial on the Great North Road at Norman Cross erected in 1914 to the men who died in the prison 1797 to 1814. The burial ground was in the field to the left of the photograph. *Author's collection*

The second prison erected was a more permanent building and was that of Dartmoor, over the main gateway of which was carved the quotation from Virgil, "Parcere Subjectis"—Spare the Humbled—and which after all this time can still be seen. Built of stone and granite, it was shaped like an enormous wheel, and the space thus enclosed was divided into two semi-circles, in one of which were the administrative buildings, and in the others, placed like the spokes of the wheel, were seven buildings for the prisoners, with a cachot or dungeon for the punishment of the recalcitrant. Then, as these were found to be inadequate to house the prisoners accumulating by reason of the continuation of the war, it was found necessary to build another prison. This, the third one, was at Perth and at one time held ten thousand of the unfortunate men.

It appears that, as these prisons were built especially for the purpose, and were rarely excessively overcrowded, the conditions in them were probably as good as, and perhaps better than, in many other places; though Dartmoor was hated by reason of its isolation, and for the fact that the damp and moorland mists, allied with the grim surroundings, made life for the prisoners harder than it might have been,[3] the prison in consequence being often referred to as "the stone tomb". But even if this is so the conditions were not as good as they should have been, nor as comfortable as they might.

3
Benjamin Waterhouse—
Journal of a Young Man of Massachusetts

Rations allowed to the prisoners

According to the printed regulations, the prisoners were to be treated fairly and even kindly, but owing to the corruption and avarice of subordinates, contractors and those in authority, many of the rules were disregarded, to the detriment of the prisoners and the enriching of those who had charge of them. The allowances were to be: on each day of the week $1\frac{1}{2}$ pounds of bread, $\frac{1}{2}$ pound of beef, mutton or other meat, substituted on two days by 1 pound of salt cod, red herrings or other fish, with potatoes and other vegetables added.

4
Louis Garneray—*Mes Pontons*

As it was an unwritten law amongst the prisoners that all should have exactly the same allowance, the rations were equally divided at each distribution, so that those who were on short rations in the punishment cells received no less than anyone else.[4] Part also was on occasions put aside for a contemplated escape and saved for those who were to make the attempt. The net result of all this was that the prisoners at no time received the full allowance with which by law they were supposed to be supplied.

But it must be conceded that much of the hardship endured by many of the prisoners was brought on themselves, to a great extent, by their gambling habits. In some cases going so far as to gamble away not only all their clothing, but also their rations for several days, so that they went naked and starving.

1.5   The great gateway of the monastery at St. Albans used as a prison during the Napoleonic wars. *Author's collection*

In Norman Cross and Dartmoor prison buildings, on each floor a treble tier of hammocks was slung from cast iron pillars for the men to sleep in; though at times when the prisons were temporarily overcrowded, the newcomers were forced to sleep on the straw which covered the floors. But, if they had money, they could do as Colonel Lebetre did when he arrived on board the hulk CANADA at Chatham in 1811—he found no sleeping place had been provided for him so he bought one for the large sum of 120 francs.

During the day the hammocks were doubled over so that both clews hung from the same hook, leaving the floor space clear, and then each bay was scoured out, though if the weather were wet a cursory sweep had to suffice. Six men constituted a mess and to each mess was issued two loaves of brown bread (whole wheat on the husk), three pounds of meat including the bone, and a handful of vegetables to be shared amongst them.

In all prisons, the men came under the jurisdiction of the Transport Office until 1817. On arrival at the depot the men were dressed in a shirt, trousers and coat, all of a saffron yellow colour; the two latter garments being stamped with the letters TO in black on front and back. One prisoner in his reminiscences complains that the coat did not meet across the chest, nor were the trousers long enough, and accuses the makers of being stingy with the cloth—but he may have been only a less fortunate recipient of government issue.

This brings us to the third method of keeping the prisoners in Great Britain. Ordinary soldiers and sailors were confined in prisons, but officers, over and above certain ranks, could choose to be put on parole. Naval men from midshipmen to commissioned officers, officers of privateers, captains and next officers of merchantmen, these were the ranks who could take advantage of the privilege.

There were five thousand men on parole in 1813, and they were usually lodged in private houses, the memory of which persists today when we hear of groups of houses referred to as Frenchman's Row or Petty France. Some parole men even lived in the prisons themselves and, in the case of those in Dartmoor, were allowed under the terms of their passes to travel to Princetown, and those in Norman Cross to Peterborough, though this was unusual.

An extremely large number of towns all over the country were used as parole towns, one of which was Bishop's Waltham where, in 1811, no less than twelve hundred prisoners lived in a block of dilapidated houses for which exorbitant rents were charged. One prisoner wrote that he paid ten shillings a week rent, not for a room but for the privilege of sleeping in a dirty garret with five other officers. So it appears that profiting from other people's misfortune is not a peculiarity of modern times.

Very strangely, included in the lists of parole towns we find the names of several ports as well, amongst which were Falmouth and Bristol; which is rather surprising when one considers the urge for all prisoners to attempt to escape, and the fact that only a stretch of water separated them from their homeland and the presence of boatmen willing to make some easy money: for the price charged for four escaped prisoners from Portsmouth to the French coast was forty pounds, that is ten pounds per head.

The parole men were required to sign a document promising, amongst other minor points, not to attempt to escape. The privileges they obtained were, and now I quote part of the actual document, ". . . liberty to walk on the great turnpike road within the distance of one mile from the extremities of the town, but that he must not go into any field or cross-road, nor be absent from his lodging after five o'clock in the afternoon during the six winter months, viz. October–March 31, nor after eight o'clock during the summer months." They were also required to report to the authorities twice a week and, as is only to be expected, their correspondence was carefully censored. Part of one letter is worth quoting but requires no comment. It was written by General d'Henin on 30 October 1804. "*Il fait de la pluie, depuis le matin jusqu'au soir, et toujours de la pluie et du brouillard pour changer. Vie de soldat ? Vie de chien !*" Under such conditions then lived, or rather existed, these men, torn from their homes and loved ones to fight for their very lives in battle; then after the war was over to find themselves cast adrift without employment, their skill in their work diminished through lack of usage, and if maimed, crippled or homeless, forced to beg for their bread in order to keep body and soul together.

Chapter 2

Types of men in enemy forces
Prisoners' pay
Formation of groups of prisoners
Activities of prisoners
Prison markets
Prison transactions

Napoleon Buonaparte can almost be said to have been the originator of total war, which we of the mid-twentieth century have experienced only too well, for the wars in which we were engaged against him affected the common people to a far greater degree than ever before, since they were themselves called on to help in the waging of it. In the days of the early 1800's it can hardly be said that Great Britain had a standing army and navy in the sense in which we know it today; for at the conclusion of a campaign, the majority of the soldiers and sailors were paid off, discharged without compensation, and left to get on as best they might. As an example of this sort of thing mention might be made of the incident recorded in the *Sunday Times* of 17 April 1853, in which we can read of a Mr. Tombleson, a petty officer who had fought on board the VICTORY with Nelson at Trafalgar. "He stated he had fought the battles of his country in 54 engagements . . . but that . . . he had been discharged without reward or remuneration saving a silver medal he wore."

The French Imperial Navy, also, was provided with crews by imposing compulsory military service, not only on sailors and fishermen on the coasts, but also on every able-bodied man, all of whom were entered on a register and divided into classes so that they could be ready to answer the summons when called on. Thus here, in the French Navy, we find men of all types, all social grades, all professions and all trades compelled to serve in the defence of their country; a system in sharp contrast to that of the British, whereby a man was enlisted by chance and only the scum of the population considered properly liable for service.

But these same men, it must be remembered, when taken prisoner were not criminals to be punished for their crimes, but enemies defeated in combat, and as such they were not treated with quite the same severity and inhumanity which characterized that meted out to the civil convicts; though, goodness knows, it was still a terrible existence. In fact, they were allowed some concessions, as will be seen. They were paid at the rate of $2\frac{1}{2}$ pence a day for an ordinary seaman, and up to 11 shillings a day for a captain, with sums ranging between these amounts for those of intermediate ranks.

When, in 1802, the Peace of Amiens was concluded, the French prisoners began to leave Great Britain as fast as transportation would allow. But the peace did not last long enough for all the prisoners to be repatriated; for, in 1812, a Frenchman named Stephen Grellet came to London. He visited French prisoners, some of whom had been recently captured, some had been in captivity since before the abortive Peace of Amiens, and in his diary he says, "I saw many of my fellow men, some of them have been prisoners for nine years and many have been brought up tenderly, even in affluence, having been conscripts that were forcibly taken from their homes, bands of whom I saw in France chained fifty or more together, dragged as sheep to the slaughter . . . some of them are content in their present bonds, under the consideration that were they liberated and sent back to France, they would soon be driven again into the army and placed in a condition worse than the present."

Now we have the picture of these prisoners in a foreign land, for such was Great Britain to the French; confined in prisons throughout the length and breadth of this country. Far from anything and anyone they knew; sojourners in a strange land; cut off from those they met, not only because they were men of a nation with whom we were at war, but also, at first, because of their inability to converse with their custodians by reason of the difference of language. In terrible isolation and the outlook uncertain, what more natural than that they should seek to alleviate their distress of mind and their solitude in some way, such as by employing their waking hours, however ephemeral and useless the result might be? For no provision was made for employment of the prisoners, they were left in idleness in each other's company with disastrous results in some cases, but beneficial in others, depending on the temperament of the man, as we shall see.

A further reason can be found in the fact that under the prison system of the day, some relief, such as extra food and little luxuries, could be purchased. So that, by making articles that could be sold, the prisoners would earn money for this purpose. As a matter of fact the prisoners were allowed to make articles for sale with the full approval, knowledge and authority of the government, for in the Parliamentary report of 25 July 1800 we can read, "The prisoners in all the depots in the country are at full liberty to exercise their industry within the prisons, in manufacturing and selling any articles they may think proper . . . and by means of this privilege some of them have been known to carry off upon their release more than one hundred guineas each." At Liverpool one prisoner took home at the Peace of Amiens three hundred guineas; and in the diary of the Rev. Robert Forby of Fincham for 25 June 1807 can be read, "Their dexterity in making toys of the bones of their meals will put many pounds into the pockets of several of them. We were very credibly assured that there are some who will carry away with them £200 or £300." As for the *Norwich Mercury* for 5 May 1814, that journal reports, "Many have realized fortunes of £500 to £1000". Incidentally, the money was also used in part to help swell the "escape fund", a phrase which requires little elucidation.[5]

5
Louis Garneray—*Mes Pontons*

Inevitably, of course, the prisoners would unconciously form themselves into groups or cliques of like intelligence and aspiration. The worst and lowest classes went by the name of Les Rafalés (rafalé is a slang French expression meaning "hard up"). A little better than them were the gamblers, Les Minables, who, it is roughly estimated, comprised half the total number in the prisons. Of a much better class were the remainder called Les Laboureurs, who, as St. Aubin, a prisoner in Portchester castle, says, knew neither reading nor writing but at least profited by their misfortunes to their own benefit ". . . *en sort sortis, la tête et la bourse passablement-meublées*". Or, in the words of Louis Garneray, also a prisoner, but on the hulks at Portchester, "I was not alone in trying to learn. Simple seamen who at first were unable to write, learnt during their time of imprisonment to express themselves adequately and to answer problems in mathematics. Some of them became almost of greater intelligence than a great many naval officers."

Lastly there were the highly educated and erudite men, Les Lords, who practised and taught their fellow prisoners the arts, crafts and knowledge of every subject with which they were conversant, through the whole gamut of Latin, Greek, tailoring, shoemaking, mathematics, algebra, dancing, boxing, painting, music, wood-carving and many other pursuits. Thus by giving lessons in these multifarious subjects the prisoners were able to earn money from their fellows. Garneray himself managed to persuade some of the guards to pay him from sixpence to a shilling for painting their portraits, and a shilling a lesson from the lieutenant for teaching his ten-year old daughter to write.

2.1 Luton plait merchants trading with French prisoners of war at Norman Cross, Huntingdonshire. Painting by A. C. Cooke. *The Museum and Art Gallery, Wardown Park, Luton*

Of a similar standard and no less praiseworthy were those who followed their own crafts or adapted their professions to the circumstances in which they were placed, becoming so successful that we find many complaints being received from the local craftsmen and workers to the effect that the prisoners and men on parole by following their own trades did so to the detriment of the legitimate traders. At Penryn the French prisoners were stopped from making confectionery for this reason, and at Norman Cross, in later years, they were prohibited from making straw plait, as it was later thrown on the market free of duty; as vouched for by the letter of Sir Rupert George to the House of Commons on 19 March 1808, wherein he writes, "I must observe that the manufactured straw plait is the only article the prisoners are prevented from manufacturing."

In Luton Museum and Art Gallery in Wardown Park, there is a painting by A. C. Cooke in which prisoners of war are shown bargaining with the market folk at Norman Cross. The commodity being sold is straw plait. Now transactions involving this article were those about which the authorities received most complaints, and so any trading in this was eventually clandestine and not done openly, a prisoner engaged in making straw plaits immediately hiding his work when the warning was received from the other prisoners that the guards were preparing to make their daily search. At the same time the picture does show certain details which even if they are imaginative are at least evocative of the industry of the prisoners, their contacts with the local populace and the activity of the markets. For instance, the man seated in the right foreground is offering for sale what is obviously a model of the block house, and perhaps finding his command of the English language rather inadequate. The actual building can be seen in the background, with one of the caserns on the left, and other buildings on the site, whilst a bare-footed girl gazes on the crippled French soldier with a look of wonder on her face. In the centre we can see two wealthy merchants bargaining for the finished straw plaits from the two eager sellers, who are clad in the ragged remains of their uniforms, and clearly trying to get as high a price as possible for their product. Standing alongside is a farmer who is no doubt waiting for the result of the transaction so that he can sell more straw to the prisoners. In the right background are booths and stalls where more trading is being done, while villagers stand about exchanging the local gossip and ever present are the British Redcoats standing on guard with bayonets fixed on their muskets.

The prisoners were permitted to dispose of their handiwork in the markets held in the prisons, under surveillance of the authorities and under strict regulations. Even the prices charged for goods required and bought by the prisoners were inspected by the agent, who was to see that they were not overcharged. One of the regulations posted up in the prison at Norman Cross reads, "Reg. 9. All dealers are to be allowed to remain at the principal gate of the prison from six o'clock in the morning until three in the afternoon, to dispose of the Merchandise to the prisoners." The market was held at the East Gate, at one period twice weekly and at another daily, and at one time even on Sundays, if we can believe Crosby's *Complete Pocket Gazette*, 1818, which reads, "Yaxley . . . to which people of all descriptions were admitted on Sundays, when more than £200 a day has been frequently laid out in purchasing their labours of the preceding week." Delegates from the prisoners met dealers from outside for traffic in their requirements, such as tools and materials for their work, and every article offered for sale in the market had to have attached to it, its price and the name of the prisoner who made it.

2.2   In the foreground are a small chest of drawers, a bottle and a small trinket box all covered in intricate straw marquetry work whilst in the background is a tea caddy decorated with cut rolled paper. *Courtesy of Arthur R. Sawers, Chicago, U.S.A.*

Dartmoor prison also had its market, as Regulation VII reads, "A market is to be held in each prison from 9 in the morning, till 12 on every day except Sunday . . . the prisoners may be enabled to purchase such articles and clothes as they may wish for, and the Agent and Officers will take care that the prisoners are not imposed upon in the prices." The market at Dartmoor was in the middle of the prison, where there was a space about one hundred feet square, Here, ranged behind long trestle tables, the prisoners sold their wares and bought goods to replenish their own needs from the people who thronged the market from the local towns such as Tavistock and Moretonhampstead: the transactions involving tobacco, needles, thread, awls, butter, eggs and soap.

At Portchester too, the Castle Yard was used once or twice a week, and here we find the commodities included straw hats, gloves, bone tobacco boxes, dominoes and chessmen, and also lace, which seems to have been peculiar to this prison. Also, as an interesting sidelight, we find some men earning money by performances of juggling, Punch and Judy shows and by the playing of musical instruments to the crowds gathered there. Certainly an ingenious idea, as no one can deny.

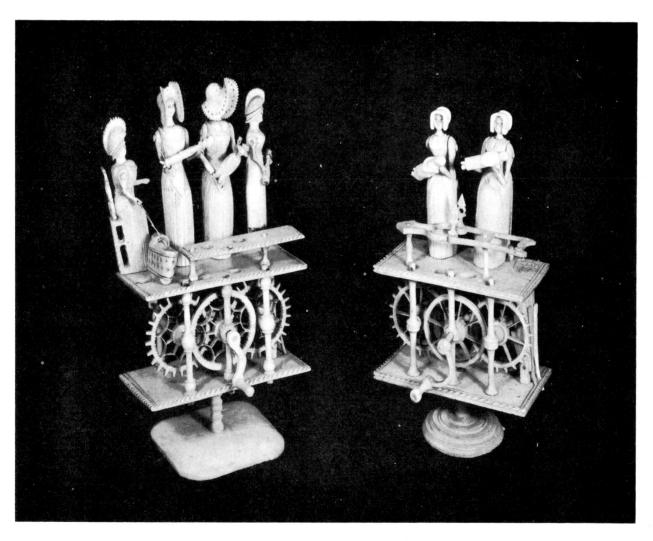

2.3 Examples of working model toys made entirely out of bone by prisoners at Norman Cross about 1805. *Courtesy of Arthur R. Sawers, Chicago, U.S.A.*

This prison was one that earned the epithet of being a hive of industry; but this could have been applied to others, for a Mrs. Grant of Jedburgh, in writing to a friend, comments in her letter thus, "The ingenuity of the French prisoners of all ranks was amazing, only to be equalled by their industry, and adding to their allowances by turning bones into neat toys eagerly bought up by all those who met with them." Or, as another writer says, "Apart from a few men, not a single one was idle. Some were planing wood, some carving chessmen or ships from scraps of bone, some were plaiting straw hats and slippers or knitting night caps. Everyone had a different craft."

Thus, as may be concluded, the prisoners came into contact with the general public of the district where they were kept and were able to obtain materials for their work and assistance in purchasing other items they needed. Certainly the tradesmen in the neighbourhood of the prisons could have no objection to the prisoners, though their reason was probably more mundane. For it is estimated that in Selkirk, the prisoners spent anything up to £150 a week, and in the two and a half years they were there, brought into the town as much as £195,000.

Luton also has reason to thank the French prisoners at Norman Cross for her prosperity of the 1900's, for A. J. Tansley, writing in the *Journal of the Society of Arts*, vol. IX, page 70, says, in reference to the invention of a simple but highly ingenious instrument for splitting the straws into finer strips, whereby the manufacturers of of the town were able to capture the straw hat trade, "It is generally supposed that the French prisoners at Yaxley Barracks, near Stilton [*sic*, i.e. Norman Cross] first made it in bone between the years 1803 and 1806."

These examples are worth remembering when we come to consider the tools and materials needed to produce the ship models, because much that is open to question and a lot that causes doubts can be explained if we admit—and it is hard to see how it can be denied—that a great deal of help must have come from outside the prisons, even to the extent of making for the prisoners certain small but intricate parts that might need the assistance of a specialized craftsman. Therefore, with this in mind, we can go on to consider the tools and equipment that it would be necessary for the prisoners to have in order to construct the wonderfully varied assortment of articles which they made for their amusement and enjoyment, and sold for their profit. So as a preliminary to this it may be of interest to discover the principal sources of the ship models and examine the evidence concerning the makers of them.

2.4 This bone model of a three-deck ship, around which are placed mirrors, is set in a case decorated with straw marquetry. This model is in the United States and exactly similar examples may be seen in the Victoria and Albert Museum, London, and Arlington Court, Barnstaple, Devon. Some bought-in material such as mirrors and glass would necessarily have been used by the prisoners to finish this. Compare this example with that in plate 8.10. *Courtesy of Arthur R. Sawers, Chicago, U.S.A.*

Chapter 3

Sources of the models
Sales of models
Prices received
Value of money
Conditions necessary for making models
Names of makers

So far I have made little mention of the ship models, not because there is no reference made to them in the many books consulted or by the many people interviewed, but so as to name as far as possible all the sources of the models together. It appears that certain prisons seem to have produced the ships in greater numbers than others, and although no one prison had a monopoly of their production, some prisons can be shown as having been the provenance of none.

One of the chief sources is claimed to have been Dartmoor where the prisoners, often referred to by Shortland the governor as "those d . . . . d frog eaters", are also stated to have made ship modelling a thriving industry. A picture is vividly conjured up for us by a writer who says that, when the hammocks were clewed up in the morning, in the bays so formed, the prisoners who bought in the markets kept shops, and those who had the necessary skill formed groups of up to six men and worked together cutting up bones and other materials to make boxes, baskets, ship models, chessmen or walking sticks of bone rings.

Another principal source of many of them is Norman Cross. In Peterborough museum is a tiny bone ship model which it is definitely stated originated from this depot; for the document attached to the model says it "was made by a French prisoner of war and bought from him by Martin of Glatton from whom it passed to his daughter Mrs. Virtue Wheatley of Whittlesey. From her it passed to the donor." The places named are villages in the locality. There are many other articles to be seen in this museum, such as bone guillotines, watch stands, cribbage boards and straw marquetry pictures. For one of these pictures, a view of Peterborough Minster, £5 was paid in 1811.

3.1   This bone model is fairly typical in that the hull is planked with bone strips, it has elaborate carving and detail work also in bone, and the bone spars are painstakingly rigged with thread of varying scale thicknesses

Common features seen here are over-scale and over-ornamented hammock nettings and rails of the head and the exaggerated length and quantity of spars such as royal masts and studding-sail booms. Notice also the stylized quarter galleries

A nice inlaid (as here) or straw marquetry base was often a feature as well as mechanism to retract the guns, the operating cord here seen projecting from the stern

This model is probably about twenty-five inches in overall length, though other models vary from as small as two inches to as much as seven feet. *Courtesy of Arthur R. Sawers, Chicago, U.S.A.*

At Portchester bone articles are said to have been made with penknives and sharpened nails, and here we are told that a bone model of a man-of-war only one foot long was sold for £26. In fact, it seems that from this prison came a very large number of the models, since the name is encountered frequently.

Liverpool was also another prolific source of the models, and from here originated many delightful miniatures, measuring only a few inches long and made of bone, ivory, wood and even straw. The prisoners were housed in the Borough Gaol in Great Howard Street, and though the prison was surrounded by a high blank wall, access to the prison appears to have been fairly unrestricted until quite late in the nineteenth century, so that the prisoners were able to dispose of their models quite openly; this fact I shall have to refer to in a later chapter. Those in the Tower prison are recorded as begging for alms of the visitors, from the barred windows of their quarters.

To a lesser degree can be named Forton near Gosport as being the source of others, for in a contemporary letter we read that an American taken prisoner at sea "went to join the other Americans who were making ship models at Forton". These, incidentally, seem to have been on a far larger scale than those made by the French, often being upwards of five feet long. In this prison also we know by the statement of Sous-lieutenant Doisy de Villargennes of the 26th French line regiment and who was on parole, that he was told by Germain Lamy, his foster brother, that he and a companion worked at a bone model of a 74 gun ship, with the rigging made of hair, for six months, and that it was sold for £40. Lamy was released in 1814 and took back with him to France 16,500 francs, which with the rate of exchange in 1811 at 24 francs to the pound sterling represents almost £700.

At Chesterfield, it is recorded, many of the bone ships were disposed of by lottery, the only clear statement of this method of selling the models. In the museum at Anne of Cleves house at Lewes is a bone model of a frigate which bears on its label the remark that it was made in the gaol in Lewes Castle.

As for the model in Dover Museum, this is a ship of which it is said, maybe apocryphally but possibly with an element of truth, that it was made by a prisoner in Dover Castle, that it was unfinished when the Peace of Amiens was signed, and though the prisoner had the opportunity to be repatriated, he declined on the ground that the model needed completing and stayed to finish it. The result was unfortunate for himself, seeing that by the time it had been finished, war had broken out afresh and so he was forced to remain in prison for a further period.

Then there is the bone model of H.M.S. TEMERAIRE of 98 guns at Wool House Maritime Museum in Southampton; this was made, it is thought, locally at the Wool House, which is referred to even now as the French Prison.

3.2 A good example of a wooden model. Being easier to work, wood ensured greater accuracy and better scale in the details. These models were often accurately painted and varnished to appear very realistic. Frequently the bottom was covered in correctly applied, but over-scale, copper sheeting. The base here is also wood. The figurehead was frequently, however, as in this case, made of bone. The ensign here is not contemporary. *Courtesy of Arthur R. Sawers, Chicago, U.S.A.*

Sometimes we find little notes attached to the models stating their place of origin. One at Arlington Court, on a three decker of 80 guns, says that it was made by a French prisoner of war at Taunton in 1818. Another on a 50 gun frigate, ten inches long, informs us that it was made by French prisoners in Milbay (*sic*) Prison, Plymouth, 1810–1812. Or again on another a note says it was made by a prisoner of war at Portsmouth in 1800. This is a miniature model of about five inches long of a 78 gun man-of-war, made of boxwood.

But it is not likely that the ship models were a main source of industry at any of the prisons, partly because the prices realized were small in comparison with the time taken to make them, allied to the fact that often more than one man helped in making them. Though the unsupported statement of a correspondent in *Ships and Ship Models* in June 1932 that they were sold "often for trifling sums of money", or the remark made by the writer in *Marine Models* in April 1933 that "they used to get a few shillings for them with which they purchased tobacco ... etc.", is not borne out by the facts, seeing that I have already referred to models sold for £26 and £40 and that contemporary writers frequently use such phrases as, "the toys were sought after"; "the turmoil of the busy prison markets"; "the products were eagerly bought up", and others of similar nature, this clearly shows that, with such a demand, there existed almost a sellers' market, and therefore, though the prices would have tended to be competitive, they would still have been inclined to be high, rather than low or trifling.

Value of money   Furthermore, though the actual sums paid may seem to us today to be low, it must be remembered that the pound sterling in the early 1800's had a far greater purchasing power and intrinsic value than at the present time. It is exceedingly difficult to give an accurate estimate of the value of money in 1800 until the end of hostilities, not only on account of the fluctuation in prices which would occur in the time of war, but also because the living conditions and the requirements of the average man were so very different from those obtaining today. But we can roughly assess the value of money by comparing wages received by workers, and it appears that a man could live reasonably comfortably on £40 or £50 a year. Thus the prices paid by the purchasers assume a very different aspect when brought into line with the present-day value of money.

Apart from the reason of time required, in some prisons the conditions were not conducive to delicate and meticulous work, and certainly because the type of man to be found there, either did not have the necessary skill and knowledge, or else was not of the temperament to undertake the work. This would be true undoubtedly of the hulks in later years, but not necessarily so at first. For, as we have seen, the types of men in the hulks were hardly such as to concentrate on tasks requiring a fair degree of mental aptitude since, as already noted, it was not long before the hulks were used for the punishment of the recalcitrant prisoners and those with criminal tendencies. This belief is strengthened when we read the following description of the inhabitants of a hulk by an eye-witness,[6] "Picture an army of corpses emerging from their graves, hollow-eyed, bent, unshaven, their faces wan and grey, their bones half covered with yellow rags."

6
Louis Garneray—*Mes Pontons*

However, we do know that in the early years one of the prisoners, whom I have already quoted, Louis Garneray by name,[7] who became an artist of international repute in private life and whose paintings surviving today are invaluable documents of contemporary life, saved money earned from other prisoners by supplying designs of seascapes, as a change from their old ones of flowers and birds, at the rate of three sous apiece, for those who made straw marquetry pictures. These were either framed or used to cover boxes of all kinds, and similar small objects,[8] and as backgrounds in the cases holding the ship models. Also in the early years of the hulks, a bone ship model at Rochester, to which I shall refer later, is reputed to have been made in the hulks at Chatham.

7
Captured March 1806, imprisoned in hulk PROTHEE, released April 1814

8
See plate 2.2 on page 18

But, generally speaking, the prisoners in the hulks would not have been the type either to take the trouble or provide the concentration necessary to make the ship models, to have the skill and patience or, most important of all, suitable conditions for the work, since the only light to reach the gun decks came from the grille-covered gun ports, and to the orlop deck from narrow scuttles. The miserable half-light from even these apertures being partly obscured by teachers explaining the mysteries of algebra and geometry to their comrades, so that apart from the difficulty of obtaining materials for their work, there was the greater difficulty of finding a place in which to work, which was as quiet as it conceivably could be and as light as possible.

"Lights out" was at eight o'clock in the winter, and nine o'clock in the summer, but these ingenious prisoners contrived to provide artificial light by saving what grease they could from their rations, placing it in an oyster shell and hanging it above the work bench.

Since the prisoners were cut off from frequent communication with the general public as sources of supply of raw materials, and for the sale of the finished product, their only means of disposing of the goods they made was through the assistance of the guards, who appear never to have been averse to trading with the prisoners, in buying the things they made and obtaining for them the goods they needed. On one occasion in 1810, as punishment for some disturbance, Lieutenant Ross of the CROWN forbade all comunication with the shore. Thus access to the bum-boats, the only other source from which the prisoners were able to buy the many things they needed or through which they could sell the goods, was denied to them.

Because, therefore, of the crowded conditions of the hulks, their inaccessibility, the dim light, and the oppressive atmosphere that was an outstanding feature, the task would be even more stupendous an undertaking than it certainly was and preclude any exact work.

It is difficult, however, to understand how much of the delicate work could have been done even in the crowded gaols of the time as has been described. I am therefore led to the conclusion that it is not unlikely that some of the best of the models were made outside the prisons by the trusted and officer prisoners who were on parole. For they would not only be able to work under more congenial surroundings, but would also be able to secure those superior tools and materials not so easily obtained by men behind locked gates.

These men on parole would also have the added advantage of being able to contact prospective purchasers of models, and in some cases would be able to obtain an order from an affectionate wife, sweetheart or fond parent who desired a model of the ship in which the loved one was serving. Obviously accuracy in these cases would not be a prime necessity, for it would have been extremely doubtful if many of this type of purchaser would have been able to recognize or even bother about errors of detail so long as the model bore a superficial resemblance to the one it was supposed to represent. To support this belief it can be stated that examples are to be found of documents attached to a model saying that it was made for a particular person.

But, alas, for fame, in spite of the fact that goods sold in the prison markets had to show the maker's name and the price, little evidence remains to connect any one particular model with any one named man. For out of the thousands of prisoners who were confined within these shores, a few names only have been recorded as being those of makers of work done in the prisons, and only of two of these do we know anything more than the name.

Though these men are not identified as builders solely of ship models, it is quite within the bounds of possibility that they may have had a hand in the making. For it would seem that very often several prisoners formed themselves into a syndicate, and by means of a concerted effort made quite a number of those models still existing, since it is possible to recognize the individual craftsman's work in more than one model with as much certainty as if he had appended his signature, and leads to the conclusion that within the groups one man would carve the figureheads, another the hammock nettings, another carved decorative bands, and so on; this I shall enlarge on in a later chapter. Otherwise, for one man to construct an exceptionally well detailed and elaborate model, whether it be a large example of two feet or more in length, or a tiny model of one and a half inches long surrounded by intricate decoration of every imaginable sort, would have taken such a length of time that the proceeds from its sale would have made their task an unprofitable one in comparison with the smaller and simpler knick-knacks that were so much more easily made.

One of these, by name Jean de la Porte, made straw marquetry pictures and designs. He was a seaman who had fought at Trafalgar and was a prisoner for nine years. Some of his work, which was done at Norman Cross, can be seen in Peterborough museum. Five others M. Grieg, Rebout, Jacques Gourny, Godfroi and Corn, are associated with the making of straw decorations and patterns, and carved bone work. A seventh name is Le Foy, a prisoner at Dorchester, whose models, it is said, can be recognized by the red, blue and gold bands on the masts and the bright colours about the ship and figurehead; but this seems to me a vague means of identification and furthermore descriptive of a great number of the models. The eighth is that of Joseph Julien Piedagnel, a prisoner at Leek from 1803 to 1814, who was "a most ingenious gentlemen, a splendid draughtsman and an artistic workman", and who, in an application for employment after his return from captivity, says he occupied his leisure during that time "with the mathematics of the design and construction of the ships".

Another is suggested by the name on the stern of a bone frigate of 80 guns in Liverpool museum; it reads LE ROUX. Now there was no ship of this name in the French Imperial Navy at this time, but it is a fairly common French name and also the name of the family of naval artists at Marseilles between 1780 and 1840; so may I hazard the fascinating conjecture that this was the name of the maker? If this is so, it is possibly the only signed model of the many that have survived. It is certain the maker was French and equally certain he did not know exactly what the Union Flag looked like, for the St. George's and the St. Andrew's crosses are blue, edged with white, red and white, while the remaining triangles are blue!

3.3 An elaborate and revealing model of a ship, the MURAT 84 guns, fitting out on a dockyard slip, surrounded by all its spars, rigging, boats and guns. See also plates 12.1–12.4. *With the permission of the Elder Brethren of Trinity House, London*

But another unusual model of the MURAT, 84 guns, in a dockyard setting in Trinity House, about which I shall have more to say, has a bone plaque at one end of the baseboard on which is engraved the words, *"Fait par Savagnac à Dartmoor"*. Lastly, apart from the

3.4 and 3.5 Facsimile of an inscription on the base of this miniature boxwood model only two inches long reads: "fait par Jean Bourg et Emanuel Creuzon au dépôt de Norman Cross à Angleterre en 1811". *The Parker Gallery, London*

name of Germain Lamy who has already been cited as a maker of ship models, there remains one further identification of the makers and this is on the base of an exquisite model two-decker ship, one and a half inches long, made of boxwood on a straw marquetry base. It was in the Parker Gallery, and beneath the model was glued a faded piece of paper on which was written, *"fait par Jean Bourg et Emanuel Creuzon au dépôt de Norman Cross à Angleterre en 1811"*.

Apart from these few, I have found no mention of other makers by name. Their identity is unknown and lost in the mists of the decades that have passed. Their only memorial is the amazing and delightful ship models they have left us. Their names and many of their secrets they have carried with them to the silent grave.

Chapter 4

Tools needed for model making
Knives and razors as weapons
Tool making
Cutting tools
Drills and carving tools
Sharpening tools
Jewellers' and watchmakers' tools
Lathes
Engraving tools

Any maker of model sailing ships will tell you that very few tools, and those of the simplest kind, are all that are needed for this popular hobby. Yet when the exhibits are examined at a ship model display, the results achieved by the prize winners might easily lead one to suppose that they had workshops equipped with all the latest machine tools that are available. Surprisingly enough, however, except possibly in the case of some of the professional model makers, and not all of these, many of the best amateurs work in their own homes, very often, to coin a phrase, on the kitchen table (the fortunate ones having a workroom of their own), but still with only simple tools, all of which could be packed into a small suitcase. Some of the more enthusiastic and ingenious amateurs have so arranged writing desks and bureaux that when they are opened a small bench is formed, with the tools held in racks and smaller articles in drawers.

To enumerate the tools and reduce them to a basic minimum, there would need to be a rule, a plane, one or two chisels of different widths, several small drills, a knife, a saw, a vice or clamp, one or two files, abrasives and a hammer, but very little else that could not be made or improvised. With these simple tools, the most exquisite and perfect models are made by men and also by women every year that passes, for their sheer delight and amusement, and as a very pleasant relaxation from their everyday work or profession. It goes without saying that these, too, must have been the tools used by the prisoners of war in constructing the ship models we are discussing.

Immediately, we are confronted with the question: where did they obtain the tools? But the answer is not far to seek, for though it might seem strange that men imprisoned and under strict guard should be

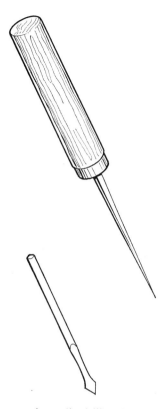

4.1 A needle drill and a spade drill

allowed to possess and use such equipment as knives and files, which could be used as offensive weapons and which we automatically associate with attempts to escape, it is nevertheless true and indisputable that these articles were in the possession of the prisoners.

As an example of this, it is known that in 1805 the Agent at Norman Cross depot, in consequence of many escapes and some unrest, for a short period impounded all implements and tools, except one knife; and that these were locked in a box during the night and then reissued the next morning. Also we have the evidence of one prisoner who, writing about the attempt he and another prisoner made to escape, describes how they forged the tools they needed by making out of knife blades, two saws, a chisel and a gimlet.

Furthermore, as I have already observed, we must not lose sight of the fact that these men were not malefactors in the accepted sense of the word. They were men who had been taken prisoner in battle, and therefore were being held temporarily by their captors, primarily for the purpose of preventing their taking any further active part in the war. The British therefore became their guardians only so long as hostilities lasted, for they were repatriated when peace was renewed. Thus they did not come under the same regulations and close confinement the civil prisoners endured.

Knives and razors as weapons

In addition, we know that many duels were fought between the prisoners themselves because of some quarrel or dispute, and that the weapons used ranged from daggers fashioned from files, and razors, to knives fastened to the ends of sticks and so used as swords, often with fatal consequences. To make these, the prisoners used the hoop iron from the casks or barrels in the prisons and forged it in the fires used for cooking purposes, or in the blacksmiths' shops attached to the prisons.

Tool making

Thus it is not difficult to see that the small tools required by the prisoners could have been and were often made by them as was necessary from either pieces of hoop iron, bolts, nails or from their knives. These materials would not be hard to acquire in the prison, for casks were the way in which many goods were usually packed, and the hoop iron bands were easily converted into knives, chisels, gouges, saws and similar cutting tools of this character. But though steel as we know it today had not been invented, the very fact of forging the iron with the use of charcoal fires automatically incorporated into the iron a small percentage of carbon and so turned it

Cutting tools

33

into a form of steel. This would be essential in the case of edge tools such as chisels and planes, and though these latter necessitated careful and precise construction they were definitely used, as I have indicated in the statement I have already quoted specifying the use of this particular tool.

Also, as we have seen, the markets were the source for the purchase of needles, from which really first-class drills can be made with the minimum of difficulty. In fact the maker of miniature ship models of today very often prefers the drills he himself makes from needles to expensive twist drills, because with them he can and does drill holes of minute diameter in the thinnest of bone or wood without fear of the material splitting. To make a drill is quite simple, the needle of suitable size is ground to a triangular section for part of its length and the other end is inserted in a wood holder, similar in thickness to that of a pencil and of any convenient length. This is then twisted rapidly backwards and forwards between the fingers, the result being that holes are quickly bored in the positions required. By filing and also by forging fine nails to shape, other types and sizes of drills can easily be made, as for instance those having diamond shaped points, a type of drill that has a very long history and is still extensively used by woodworkers, metalworkers and by jewellers as well.

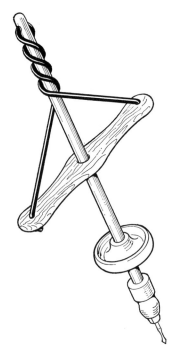

4.2 A jeweller's Archimedean drill

A more elaborate drill holder, though of ancient origin, is as easily made, and is used even today by craftsmen of various trades, including jewellers. This is the Archimedean drill, in which a cord attached at its centre to the upper end of the drill holder, winds and unwinds around it by working a cross-bar, to which the ends of the cord are fastened, up and down the central rod. Once started (a knack soon acquired), the drill itself, which is fixed into a chuck at the lower end, can be rapidly spun backwards and forwards, but not of course with a continuous rotary movement in one direction.

Nails too were undoubtedly utilized to be fashioned into small tools such as scrapers, scribers, chasers and gravers which, though we might consider them primitive and vastly inferior to the modern high-speed steel tools, could nevertheless produce almost as good a result, when in the expert craftsman's hands of which there were many as we shall see, as the orthodox tools.

But the one universal tool of all sailors of sailing ship days was the knife. It served him not only as a tool for his trade or his defence, but also for use at meal times, and in his leisure he made with it, as

Herman Melville said in 1850, "skrimshander articles, as the whalemen call the numerous little contrivances they elaborately carve out of the rough material, in their hours of ocean leisure. Some of them have little boxes of dentistical looking implements specially intended for the skrimshandering business. But in general they toil with their jack-knives alone; and with that almost omnipotent tool of the sailor they will turn you out anything you please . . . with marvellous patience, and with . . . his one poor jack-knife, he will carve you out a bit of bone sculpture . . . as close packed in its maziness of design, as the Greek Achilles's shield."

As for sharpening the tools, this must have presented little difficulty, for since there were carpenters working about the prisons, grind-stones and hones would have been within the reach of any prisoner needing to use them (in this connection note Samuel Booth's state-ment in the next chapter), and if the modern glass- and garnet-paper had no counterpart amongst the prisoners, it was not an insuperable obstacle, for fine sand makes an excellent substitute, and pieces of broken glass splendid scrapers; used even by the present-day artisan to produce a smooth surface. This too must have been available to the prisoners.

Finally as regards vices and clamps; it would require little imagination to rig up some sort of fixing device with strips of wood and wedges to be used for this purpose, and hammers, however rough, could just as easily be made.

With these tools all the constructional work on a model ship can be done if it is of a fairly straightforward and reasonably unelaborate style. Thus we can see that the tools necessary for the prisoners to make their models were neither impossible nor exceedingly difficult to obtain.

But in many of the models the ship is decorated with a multitude of carvings of most intricate design. To accomplish these, something more than the simple and somewhat crude tools I have mentioned would be necessary. Therefore, we must remember the important fact, that though warfare was in the transitional stage from a gentle-manly affair to that of mass murder, traditions of the previous ages still survived. We read of Englishmen and women travelling on the Continent at a time when we were at war with many of the countries of Europe. The postal service, such as it was, still operated. Even prisoners on parole were allowed to travel home to their native lands, on condition they did not give any aid to their own country by re-joining the fighting forces, unless notification was received that they had been exchanged for someone of equal rank, and that they would return to imprisonment in England if so ordered; their word was their only bond!

Thus when we see the delicate and intricate carving on the bows, the stern and the side galleries of the larger models, which it is evident would be well-nigh impossible to carve with penknives and nails, I am sure that this was done with special craftsman's tools such as were used by jewellers, jet carvers, ivory workers, watchmakers, or cameo and intaglio experts. These tools could undoubtedly have been purchased through the dealers who visited the markets, as I have already described.

To enlarge on this argument, look at the carved bone work in the museum in Peterborough. There you will see elaborately carved and pierced bone clock cases and small sweetmeat trays of such incredible loveliness that it is only too clear that special tools would be required. The carving is not merely of shallow scratches to simulate bas relief, but deeply sculpted to form faces, heads, flowers and interweaving leaves; and the pierced sides and bases of the trays (almost of paper thickness) are so delicate that they resemble fine lace. I have been assured that the tools for this work were sent for, by the prisoners themselves, from their home towns; and certainly this is possible, for we know that they were allowed to augment their meagre incomes by exercising their trained hands on the improvised materials they used, and that these men were conscripted from all walks of life and would in peacetime have been workers in the aforementioned crafts, and of course have business friends and associates in their homeland.

The only exception that can be made to these statements is that some of the fittings in some of the models show signs of having been made in a lathe. I have no evidence that there were lathes in the prisons; and even if there were, it is questionable if the prisoners would have been allowed to use them.

But in some specimens of prisoner work, are turned parts that so clearly have been made on a machine that a likely explanation is possible in the suggestion that in the markets, portions of bone or wood, carefully prepared for the lathe by the prisoners, were handed out to the village turner to be finished off. On the other hand, if we examine the baseboard of a model ship which is surrounded by small

4.3 A gun three-quarters of an inch long

4.4 A carronade thirteen-sixteenths of an inch long

4.5 A swivel gun eleven-sixteenths of an inch long

These are enlarged photographs of guns taken from prisoner of war ship models. At first sight they appear to have been turned on a lathe, but closer inspection reveals that all the shaping and relief work must have been made with files. *Author's collection*

balusters, rarely are they exactly similar or perfectly cylindrical; proving without doubt that some parts were laboriously carved and filed one by one. Some of the guns, too, which at first sight appear to have been turned, when examined under a powerful glass show the scratches and marks of a file, and the hole at the muzzle end is seen to be off centre. These also, therefore, have been filed up by hand one by one; consider the magnitude and tedious repetition involved in the task when the model under construction was a ship of the line of 120 guns, with added armaments such as swivel guns that had to be pivoted and mounted on the bulwarks and fighting tops!

4.6   On closer inspection the guns of this model appear to have been turned in a lathe. The bores have been drilled afterwards and in many cases are not absolutely central and are of varying sizes. *R. Creagh-Osborne*

Yet it must be admitted that some also bear signs of having been spun in some sort of primitive lathe, and many examples are extant, as for instance small balusters, cappings to pillars, knobs to handles, corner pediments and in particular a bone tobacco stopper, now in Peterborough museum, which is so symmetrical, and chased with fine circular bands, that one can say that such a finish could only have been achieved by turning in a lathe.

However, to make some sort of mechanism for revolving the work so that it could be shaped by a hand-held tool would not have been impossible; two arrangements are quite feasible, both based on the same idea and, as a matter of fact, in use today, one in the furniture trade, the other by jewellers. The chair-leg makers in the beech woods around High Wycombe still use a pole lathe, the type where a cord passes from the treadle, once or twice around the work which is held between centres, and then upwards to a spring bar. On depressing the treadle the work revolves and the cutting tool is held to the surface of the material being worked upon. When the treadle is released the spring bar lifts it and so the work is made to rotate in the opposite direction, at the same time the cutting tool is drawn back. To see an old craftsman at work in the woods is to marvel at his skill in using such a primitive apparatus, the pattern of which can be traced back to Egyptian times five thousand or more years ago. Jewellers use a similar principle of turning between centres but in their case a turns bow is used. This is a thin strip of whalebone or cane used to rotate the mandril of a lathe or an arbor by coiling a line of gut or horsehair, attached to its extremities once round a ferrule or pulley on the object rotated; again the cutting can be done only whilst the work is revolving towards the operator.

4.7   These are examples of bone work made by prisoners of war at Norman Cross. - They were obviously made in a lathe and certainly by an expert, as evidenced by the spiral fluting of the columns, the delicate plain turning and the hollowing out of the cups. *Courtesy of Arthur R. Sawers, Chicago, U.S.A.*

Another, and probably better, method would have been to hold the work being shaped in a chuck, or some similar holding device attached to a pulley. By means of a belt or cord passing around a larger driving wheel and the smaller pulley wheel, the work could be rotated continuously in one direction. Another prisoner would supply the manpower to turn the driving wheel to which would be attached a handle, whilst the expert turner applied his tools to the piece of bone or other material in the chuck and formed it to the required shape.

All these methods are perfectly feasible, and if a visit is paid to the mechanical tools gallery of the Science Museum in London, contemporary lathes of the three types I have described, and the drills as also described, may be seen together with specimens of the work performed on them, and it will be appreciated how basically simple the whole operation of drilling and turning really is. The skill comes only with practice.

Though some of the work may have been done outside the prisons by the local craftsmen, the fact that the prisoners were able to have in their possession and use, plant, equipment and tools for forging banknotes, shows that there was an absence of any but the most superficial surveillance. For when the one pound note was introduced in the last decade of the eighteenth century, forging from the first was a source of great worry and trouble to the authorities. Many instances are on record of prisoners of war bribing their gaolers with forged banknotes. So it must be admitted that if fine engraving tools, pens and brushes could be in the possession of the prisoners for this nefarious purpose, they would also have used similar tools for the more honest purpose of making toys, pictures, models and all the various articles that came from the prisons; and which can be seen in all their complexity in the museum at Peterborough, which houses what is probably the finest collection of prisoner work in Great Britain.

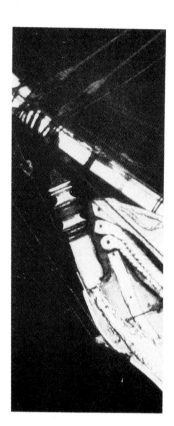

4.8 This unusual, and perhaps unique, bone figurehead was obviously made on a lathe. The impression it gives, when looked at with the rest of the model (see plates 7.15 and 7.16), is that it is not original since, apart from the lathe work, it does not match the excellent carving elsewhere. One would have expected a carved figurehead on a model of this quality.

However, it is painted in contemporary colours and one is tempted to guess that it might have been hurriedly substituted for a missing figurehead, perhaps originating as a piece of balustrade or a chess piece. *From a private collection*

Chapter 5

Varieties of materials used
Bone, baleen, ivory, tortoiseshell
Wood, wire, sheet metal, gold, silver
Cotton, thread, rope making, hair
Paints, brushes, straw
Rigging
Skilled craftsmen

The prisoners have shown remarkable ingenuity in using many unusual materials in their work. Some of the substances, of course, are those that readily lend themselves to ship model making, but there are others, as I shall show, which at first sight appear to be unsuitable and even useless, but which, due to the cleverness of the prisoners, have been applied successfully to a profitable use. The principal materials comprised, amongst others, the following: bone, ivory, tortoiseshell and similar animal substances; woods of various kinds; metals, both base and precious; glass, fibres of various vegetable origins; hair, paper, cloth, tinsel, straw, grass, dyes and pigments. These must be considered in some detail and an effort made to trace their sources, which in some cases is quite easy but in others rather obscure.

Bone If, then, a start is made with bone it will be as well to describe the general characteristics of the structure of bones, for the better understanding of the difficulties and problems which confronted the prisoners in using them. A bone is not solid in the same way as the branch of a tree or a metal rod, for though the outside is smooth and hard, below the thick surface lies an interior of a cellular construction. So that flat bones are not solid throughout and in the case of certain bones of a cylindrical form, as for instance the femur, the ends take the shape of enlarged knobs inside of which we find the cellular core extending some distance from the ends. The shaft itself is virtually hollow, though in life filled with marrow, a combination of blood cells and fat. So that though a bone may be, say, twelve inches long, the portion that would be of any use could be possibly no more than six inches, and this itself would be in effect a bone tube of which the hole might be a third of the diameter. Therefore we are left with a thin bone cylinder, out of which has to be cut flat bone strips, some

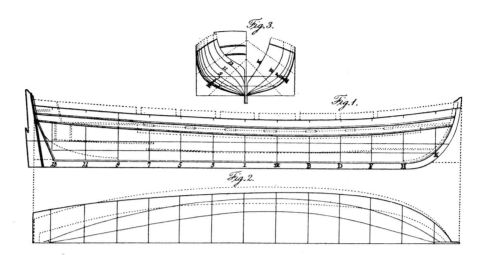

5.1 and 5.2 Two views of a bone model of a ship's boat three and three-quarter inches long which used to accompany a model that was later damaged. The thwarts are cut out of a separate piece of bone. Note the piece let into the keel because of the limitation in the size of the bone block.
R. Creagh-Osborne

A comparison with the contemporary draught of a ship's boat shows how accurate were some of the best of these models even though almost certainly shaped from memory alone.
Falconer's Marine Dictionary

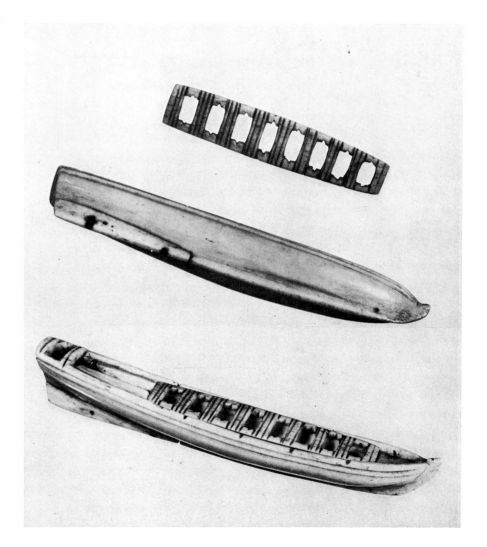

straight, some curved. This is obviously neither a very easy nor simple task; nor let it be said, a very pleasant one; for if any one has attempted the work of cutting up and shaping bone he will know what to expect. But he who does not will be repelled by the smell as the bone is sawn, scraped or filed, and reminding him of charnel houses.

Another complication also presents itself, for though a bone might appear to be straight, actually it is not so; but curves in one and sometimes two directions, so the problem is even more difficult. This accounts for the fact that usually the bone planking of a hull or a deck is made up of short strips, laid end to end; and that the masts are made the required length by pieces scarfed together. So that when we find long, straight and flat strips, they are so exceptional as to be be extremely rare.

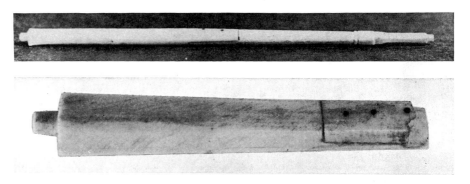

5.3 and 5.4   In order to make up sufficient length, pieces of bone were scarfed and riveted together with copper or brass wire

The upper photograph shows a lower mast with a scarfed joint mid-way along it. At the left-hand end is a tenon for fitting into a hole in the deck. At the right-hand end is the masthead carved and shaped to receive the top, and at the extreme end, the cap. This spar is five and three-quarter inches in length. The broken piece below is just under two inches long. For a further example see plate 6.18. *With permission of Mr. A. Ebelthite, Author's collection*

However, there was an almost unlimited supply of bone, for as I have shown each prisoner was allowed each week upwards of five pounds of meat including the bone; and when we consider that at Dartmoor, for instance, there were anything between three and six thousand men at various times during the period the prison was in use, the amount of meat that was consumed at this depot alone was enormous. A butcher has computed that on an average five or six bullocks would be required each day to feed the prisoners, and therefore the quantity of bone would be prodigious. But since the actual amount of bone required for model-making purposes would be relatively small, the prisoners could afford to be prodigal of the

5.5 and 5.6 Examples of finely detailed carving of objects made entirely in bone. Above is a companionway seven-eighths of an inch square, whilst below is a skylight one and three-eighths inches long by seven-eighths of an inch wide. *With permission of Mr. A. Ebelthite*

9
Examples of this style can be seen in many of the photographs. Note particularly those in plates 6.13 and 6.21

10
As can be seen in plates 6.14–6.18 and 6.21

quantity available, and use only that which exactly suited the requirements of the article under construction. Germain Lamy at Forton, who has already been mentioned in a previous chapter, stated that, "beef bones and mutton bones were kept on all sides, those that could not work selling them at good prices to those who could". So we see there was a regular traffic in this material and that the choicest and most suitable pieces were of some value.

There is a large variety of bone amongst the models. Beef bone is the most common because of the greater quantity which was available as compared with that from other animals and other meats such as mutton, veal and whale. Undoubtedly in the extremely large bone models of around five feet long, whalebone was the variety used. For we find exceptionally large pieces which could have come only from the whale, as for instance a strip forty inches long, one inch wide and one eighth of an inch thick, which is used as the sole plate or false keel to the keel of the model in Watermen's Hall, and in which model also, the yards are each of one piece of anything up to thirty inches long. Some of the smaller models are decorated Nelson style, that is by dark wales between the gun ports.[9] These are occasionally made of white bone dyed black, the colour of which has tended to fade or become mottled in the course of time. More usually, and with a much better effect, black[10] or dark brown baleen is used, which is a product of the whaling industry. Sometimes tortoiseshell is used instead, but this is not so common.

The mouth of the true whale has no teeth but contains plates of a hornlike substance called baleen, which is usually of a very dark colour tending to be almost black, and through which the animal strains its food. Formerly whalebone was one of the prizes of the whaling industry and much used at that time when ladies' fashions and rigid corsets created a demand for the substance, apart from its use by the manufacturers of umbrellas, parasols and coach-hood frames, and of course by the brush trade. Today the position is rather different with plastics taking the place of bone in so many instances and making whalebone hardly worth the trouble of marketing it, except by crushing it to make soil fertilizers.

A notable feature of the bone ship models is the whiteness of the bone where the model is in its original case or where it has been carefully protected during the decades that have passed from dust and grime. A partial mystery of all the bone articles is how this whiteness was achieved because bone straight from the animal has a high fat content and soon becomes not only dirty but also of a yellowish hue. So the first thing that had to be done to make the bones white was to boil them and so remove as much of the fat and the glue-forming substances as was possible. This in itself was a necessary by-product for the prisoners in their activities, for glue must have been in constant demand by all the workers. But merely boiling alone does not whiten the bones sufficiently, so it is then imperative to bleach them. There are several ways in which this can be done: firstly, by exposure to sunlight, which is a slow and lengthy process; secondly, by the action of sulphur dioxide. Sulphur was used in all the prisons as a disinfectant, and, if it is burned in the vicinity of water, dilute sulphuric acid is formed, which acts as a bleaching agent; thirdly, the straw plait merchants used to bleach their straw by using hydrogen peroxide, so we can assume that this chemical could have been procured by the prisoners; fourthly, by the use of lime, another easily obtained substance used in the prisons. This will also act as a bleaching agent when used in the form of a wet paste or a solution; lastly, by soaking in a lye of potashes, a bleaching action is obtained.

After this length of time it is impossible to say with any certainty what method was used, but undoubtedly one of these methods or a variation of them would have been necessary and could have been used, the bone afterwards being scraped to smooth the surface. All of these bleaching processes, it is conjectured, would have taken place after the bone had been converted to convenient sizes for constructional work, because it would then be fresh and during the process softened and made pliable enough to take up the curves of the shape of the hull. However, if bone is soaked in aromatic vinegar it can be made pliable to a certain degree, though bone is in itself elastic when cut into thin strips since it is used in this way by savages for the making of bows.

Ivory

Ivory is rarely used; a great many models described as being made of ivory are in actual fact bone, but there are some specimens which are genuine ivory.[11] However, the source of this material, as well as tortoiseshell, is a problem of its own. It is difficult to see how this substance was available to the prisoners except with the help of people outside the prisons from whom it could be bought, and with whom, as I have shown, they had much contact. And a suggestive point is raised when we read that in Liverpool, an ivory carver living in Dale Street was arraigned before the justices for assisting a prisoner to escape.

11
However, see the description on page 90 and also plate 7.8 of an ivory model

5.7   H.M.S. CERES, an 18 gun frigate to a scale of 1 : 96. Made in Howard Street, Liverpool, prison about 1785, probably commissioned by a Liverpool citizen. One of the rare models in which the hull planking is made of tortoiseshell, the rest being in bone. These details were supplied by Lieutenant-Commander J. H. Craine in whose possession the model was at one time

A note below the bow reads "Built Liverpool 1781 Fearn & Webb (later completed by Grayson). Re-fitted Deptford 1792 and cut down from 36 to 18 guns. Present at the taking of Martinique (Sir John Jervis) 1794 and at San Domingo 1796. Broken up 1830." *Courtesy of Arthur R. Sawers, Chicago, U.S.A.*

Therefore, we can readily assume that here was a source of this substance for the prisoners, since ivory has always been in great demand for the making of boxes, combs and chessmen, and was not so scarce as to be excessively priced. That the prisoners did obtain ivory is proved by the trade card of one of the prisoners on parole at Leek. He was a privateer officer, and the card reads, "James Francis Neau. Derby Street. Leek. Sells straw hats, ivory and bone articles made by the French prisoners".

It is likely that tortoiseshell as well would be available from a similar source, used as it was for the making of combs, ornamental head dressings, boxes and other decorative purposes. Fish bones, too, were occasionally used and are to be seen principally in the miniature models, in this class of model is also used mother-of-pearl, many tons of the shell being imported every year from Manila into Liverpool. Horn is also used but very rarely, and then it has been treated in such a way as to disguise its real nature, which will be explained and dealt with in a succeeding chapter.

Wood As for wood, this must have been available in almost unlimited quantities, since much timber was used in the construction, repair and heating of the prisons. A man named Samuel Booth said that his grandfather, by name Samuel Briggs, who was a carpenter, went to work at times to Norman Cross, and that the prisoners used to beg pieces of wood and (this is worth noting) other substances from him. Thus would be obtained the commoner varieties of timbers such as the firs or pines which would be used in building construction. But I will quote an extract from the Diary of Archdeacon Strong, on the date 23 October 1801, to show another source. "Drove Margaret to the Barracks [Norman Cross]. Bought the model of the Block House and provided the Mahogany, £1 11 6. Sergt. 1 shilling, Man 1 shilling, Soldier 1 shilling and 3 pence." It is likely the last three sums were gratuities, and I expect the one and a half guineas paid to the prisoner were in gold coins. But the reason for quoting the extract is that it shows that not only were materials supplied by the purchasers of the finished articles, but that they were sometimes commissioned by the purchaser as well. Thus many of the less common woods such as box, mahogany, lime and walnut would come into possession of the prisoners from outside sources.

Many metals would be available in the ways cited in the previous pages, and this applies to the more common base metals such as iron, brass and copper, some of which could have been found lying about the prisons. But much of this, in the form of wire or sheet metal, would undoubtedly have had to be purchased in the prison markets, for wire and sheet metal is frequently seen to have been used in the models. Often the planking and decking of a model is not fixed with nails as at first appears, but with what is obviously wire, hammered into a previously drilled hole and riveted over. This is the usual method of fixing the scarfed joints of a mast, and for pinning the planking of the decks to the deck beams, or of the hull sides to the frames if the hull is built-up.

Wire was also used for the making of rudder chains or for eye-bolts. Actually this is not a difficult task, for if a length of wire is wound

5.8 Though some models were made entirely of wood, this model is somewhat unusual in having basically a bone-planked hull, but the upper part of the stem and the beak head are made of wood quite elaborately painted. The model also has wooden spars and upper work details. *R. Creagh-Osborne*

around a rod of suitable size, the spiral so made can then be cut lengthwise and thus converted into split rings, which have only to be linked together to make chain; which again is the way many expert ship model makers of today make chain to scale sizes, from remarkably small links up to studded chain cable for the anchors of present-day battleships. Oval link chain, of course, can easily be made by squeezing the round links between a pair of pliers either before or after assembly; and a reprint of an article on the making of small chain for ship models can be read in *Model Boats* for September 1969, page 389.

5.9 Chain from a prisoner of war ship model. The links are actually one-sixteenth of an inch in diameter. *Author's collection*

Many models are to-be seen in which the hull below the water line is covered with copper sheet, in imitation of the custom of the day before the invention of anti-corrosion paints, of plating the lower part of the hull with sheets of copper or yellow metal (called Muntz metal after its inventor) about four feet long and one foot wide.[12] This was done to protect the planking of the hull from the depredations of the teredo worm which bored into the wood leaving an empty track behind to such an extent that, when one sees in a museum a piece of worm-eaten timber, one wonders how a seriously infected ship held together. It is unlikely that this sheet metal could have been obtained except from an outside source.

12
See the example in plate 9.1 on page 115

Gold and Silver

But some models bear fittings of silver or sometimes of gold, as well as of brass and copper, and these precious metals came from several sources, such as from the personal ornaments of the prisoners. Finger rings and also earrings were worn by the sailors of those days and in addition to any keepsake they might possess, it must not be forgotten that gold coins were current tender. The values minted in the reign of George III were of one, half, third and quarter guineas; and in the reign of George II the gold coins were of five, two, one and half guineas. All these, whether ornaments or coins, were beaten out in the way the gold beater works, to provide thin plates of metal which were then cut up to the necessary sizes for fixing in the positions required. Gold coins appear to have been used at this time for many purposes other than that for which they were intended, for we can read that the gold coins in circulation became very much diminished in value by filing, clipping and other malpractices, while those issued new from the mint were often melted down and exported.

However, there are fittings which at first sight appear to be of gold, and are often stated as being gold, such as mast bands, rudder pintles and gudgeons, and other small parts, but which are not real gold at all, but actually metal foil backed with paper (similar to that used today to wrap chocolates and toffees), which has been cut to size and then glued in place; in the same way that was done a few decades later by our Victorian forefathers in making tinsel pictures, and for adorning the characters of the "penny plain, tuppence coloured" model theatres of their childhood.

As for the remaining materials I have mentioned, we can trace a source in the stores kept in the prisons, for we can read in a letter

5.10 Deck details from a wooden model showing two binnacles in front of the wheel and a compass on top of a binnacle by the sailor. Note the overscale size of the grating holes, almost as large as the deck planking which is approximately to scale. See also plate 10.4. *The National Maritime Museum, Greenwich*

from the government to John Delafons, the first Agent to Norman Cross, on 18 March 1797, a list of official stores and comprising amongst other things, "Large Twine 6 doz., Small Twine 4 doz., Tow 50 lbs., Paint, Turps, Oil, White Brown Thread 8 lbs., and Jute for the prisoners to make their own hammock lanyards". The standing and running rigging of the model ships, where not of hair, is made of cotton or thread and is laid either right-handed or left-handed according to the particular purpose for which it was required. This obviously proves that these miniature ropes and cables were made by the prisoners themselves who, if sailors, would unquestionably have the knowledge and skill to make up rope.

Rope making

The knowledge, art and practice of rope making, knotting, splicing and fancy work was an accomplishment which the seamen of sailing ship days were not only required to possess, but one of which they could justly be proud. For apart from the necessity of being able to assist in the rerigging of the ropes of ships that had been damaged by stress of weather or by being shot away in battle, they would also need to know how to make up new rope from old, and to make the decorative rope work about the ship such as bell ropes, ropes for gangways and accommodation ladders, pointed ends to ropes for reeving through blocks, fancy knots to the ends of ropes to act as stoppers, and for their own amusement the beckets for their lockers; regrettably, an art that exists today, to a great degree, only in books. But, as I have shown, they had to make up their own hammock lanyards, and indeed, were provided with the raw material to enable them to do so.

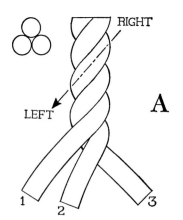 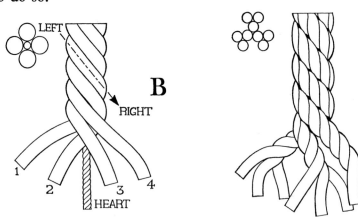

5.11 A.   Three strands laid up to form a right-handed rope. Called *Hawser* laid.
B.   Four strands laid up (usually with a heart) to form a left-handed rope used for shrouds and stays. [*Shroud* laid rope (a confusing term) is four strands laid up right-handed and not necessarily used for shrouds].
C.   Three, three-stranded, right-handed ropes laid up to form a nine-strand left-handed cable. Called *Cable* laid.

The hair, with which many of the miniature ship models are rigged, came, of course, from the prisoners' own heads or from their pig-tails, another fashion of the sailors of those days; or in the larger models rigged with hair, when thicker and longer lengths would be required, horse hair is the material used, and of this was made, especially at Dartmoor prison, many curious articles such as hair bracelets, finger rings and necklaces.

Paints   The dyes and pigments must have come principally from the villagers and dealers in the markets, not, as has been asserted, from the clothes of the prisoners which they soaked in water to extract the dye (a fantastic idea), nor from tea (an even more fantastic idea), for what colour can one get from tea except brown, and which in any case was in those days the beverage of the well-to-do classes by reason of its cost, and not the common drink of the general populace? Yet there are examples of prisoner work in many museums, of pictures of country scenes painted in bright colours on paper, and stuck to the insides of the lids of boxes; and in Peterborough, one of a line of red-coated soldiers in the regimental accoutrements of the day, framed in wood. Also are to be seen straw marquetry pictures where the sky is not of inlaid coloured straws, but painted on afterwards, over the natural buff colour of the straw; though in some cases to be described later the straw has been dyed.

5.12 A is a dead-eye, B is a bull's-eye. This drawing also shows, as if looking from outboard, how a shroud is set up when the cordage is either right- or left-handed.

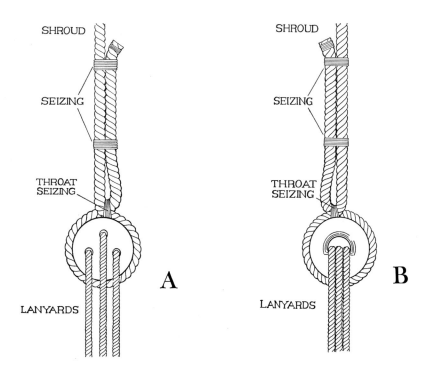

Fig. 4.

These examples must have necessitated the use of brushes as well, which could have been made from human hair (though if you do make a brush in this way, it does not make a very good substitute for bristles), but more likely were purchased in the markets. Garneray, who has already been referred to, states that he got into touch with an English tradesman who, for nine guineas, supplied him with a box of colours with several large sheets of paper, brushes and pencils. Another prisoner said that he managed to acquire enough cash to be able to buy proper brushes, oil colours and canvas.

The straw with which many delightful pictures, the baseboards and some boxes are covered, came from the straw which covered the floors and was also brought into the prisons by the local farmers and tradesmen for the making of straw plait. This straw subsequently had to be smuggled into the prisons, as we have seen, and is the only material I have been able to discover that was smuggled in. For, in spite of the general belief that many goods illegally reached the prisoners, on account of the freedom of the markets there was no need to smuggle goods in, though there was a traffic in goods smuggled out of the prisons, including forged banknotes and passes. But sometimes, instead of straw, grasses were used and these were picked by the prisoners on the *prés* or airing grounds of the prisons.

It is extraordinary that though the prisoners were usually closely and strictly guarded, at times this was relaxed to an astonishing degree. For instance, on one occasion several prisoners from a hulk were subpoenaed to appear at the trial ashore of one of their compatriots who had been arrested on a charge of forgery of banknotes. One of the prisoners in recounting the story says that they then had the opportunity of "buying some of the things we needed, tools and so on".

5.13 This contemporary drawing shows how a lower shroud was rigged and connected via dead-eyes (d) and lanyards (c) to the chain wales (f) and chains (g) then to the chain plate (h) nailed to the side of the ship. Note that a draughtsman's error shows the rope changing from right-handed to left-handed as it alters its direction. A left-handed rope remains left-handed whether it goes up or down! *Falconer's Marine Dictionary*

5.14 This detail photograph shows the lower ends of the shrouds of a typical model. At the top the main shrouds are made of rope which should be laid left-handed (see also plate 4.6). Between the dead-eyes are the lanyards which are laid right-handed. Below the dead-eyes and between the chain wales and the ship's side the modeller has used twisted wire instead of elongated chain links which would have been correct (see drawing 5.13). The ratlines are correctly clove-hitched to the shrouds. *R. Creagh-Osborne*

Does this mean that they were actually allowed to enter shops to purchase the goods in the same way a prisoner on parole might do? If so, one must conclude that they did so with the connivance of the soldiers who had been detailed to escort them to and from the hulk.

In all the foregoing we should not forget that this took place over a century and a half ago, before the Industrial Revolution, and when most work was done by hand; when skilled craftsmen were as common as they are rare today; when women were expert in needlecraft and every man trained from boyhood to use his hands; for few could rely on machines to produce a desired result. Thus, though we gaze with wonder (and rightly so) on the works of many unknown and long-forgotten peasant craftsmen, we should try to view in the right perspective the difference in present-day conditions, and attempt to realize, but with due credit and praise, that what we might consider today as hard work and tedious toil, was an ordinary procedure in the days when machines were a dream of the future, but handcraft a common achievement.

5.15   A French 110 gun ship. Thirty-nine inches in length overall. A splendid example of pierced bone work for decoration as opposed to the more usual carved work. Note also that the woolding on the masts are finished with hoops above and below each band. *The U.S. Naval Academy Museum, Annapolis, U.S.A.*

Chapter 6

The methods used in the construction of the ship models are neither different from those that have been used for centuries, nor are they different from those used at the present time by all ship model makers. Examples of the various methods are usually to be seen made of either bone or wood, or in a combination of the two, and are comprised of the following:

A. Built-up models.
B. Solid hulls.
C. Hulls solid up to the gun deck, framed above.
D. Solid hulls hollowed out down to the gun deck.
E. Solid hulls cut longitudinally, with a central keel plate.

To make these methods clearer, a brief description of them will be of assistance to those who are not familiar with the techniques of ship model making, and of use in identifying each method.

Built-up models
The built-up models are the least numerous and are usually only those of the largest size. Without doubt this method demands the most care in the making and calls for the exercise of all the skill of which the workman is capable. This way of making model ships is based on the method the shipwrights used in the construction of the full-size ships in which the keel is laid first on the launching slipways, and to it, at each end, are fastened the stem and sternpost.

Across the keel, vertically and at right angles, are fixed the frames, these are made of wood of the shape of the section of the hull at many points along its length. When all the frames are in place, planks of wood of suitable width and thickness are then bent horizontally around the frames and fixed to them with wood dowels, called treenails, usually starting from the keel and working upwards. After the hull has been completely planked, the deck beams are fixed and finally the decks are laid. In a model, the principle is the same but with some modifications to simplify the method for model-making purposes; for instance, in a real ship the frames are made of several pieces of wood scarfed together and have a gap of only a few inches between them. In a model the frames may be made of one piece of wood, and there will be far fewer of them. Though it is not necessary to have so many, they must be fairly close together, otherwise, when the planks are bent around the frames, instead of a nice gentle curve being formed, the planking will lie as a series of flats from frame to frame. Both sides are done simultaneously to prevent the hull from being forced out of shape, and becoming asymmetrical. In this method once the hull is planked the model assumes the appearance of a real ship.[13]

13
A superb example of a hull that is accurate as to scale and detail is the 46 gun heavy frigate shown on page 125, plate 10.3

Solid hulls All the other methods are model makers adaptations and bear little relationship to full-size practice since they are based on the principle of carving a solid block of wood to the shape of the hull and fixing imitation planks to it, as I shall describe later. The solid block may be one thick piece of wood, or else composed of several planks glued together to make up the thickness and length required, and then sawn

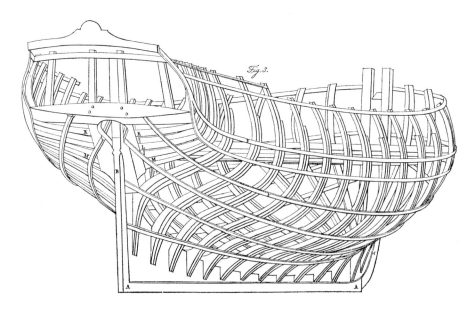

6.1 A contemporary drawing from Falconer's *Universal Dictionary of the Marine* shows how the framing of a typical small ship was built up

6.2   The hull of this model is solid to the top of the upper deck and the grain of the painted wooden core can be clearly seen in the gun ports at the right. The gun barrels are simply pushed into holes in the core. Note the poor fitting of the planking, no gun port lids and the inferior imitation rigging using knots and beads, though left-handed rope has correctly been used for the shrouds. *R. Creagh-Osborne*

to the shape of the plan view of the hull. Surplus wood is removed with chisels or gouges and, by means of templets of card, metal or thin wood, of the shape of the section of the hull at several points along the keel, which are offered up to the hull as the carving proceeds, the block is formed into the shape of the hull; both sides in this instance, also, being done simultaneously. When the outside has been smoothed off to the correct shape, the inside is sometimes gouged out until the sides are of uniform thickness, but in the case of method B, the hull is left as a solid (see plate 6.2), and grooves are cut to take the keel, stem and sternpost which are then glued in place.

In method C, the hull is solid only up to the gun deck, that is, the deck for the lowest line of guns, above which it is built up, as in method A, but with only the upper parts of the frames, i.e. from the gun deck to the top rail of the bulwarks, and then covered with planks on the outside.

6.3 Example of a solid hull hollowed out to the main gun deck level. The objects within the hull are part of the gun-retracting mechanism. For further details of this, see later in this chapter. The white projections on each side are chain wales to take the lower shrouds. *W. H. Honey*

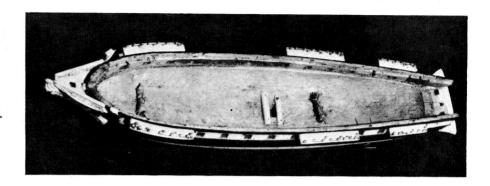

In method D, the hull is made solid and then hollowed out, but only down to the gun deck, the gun ports being cut in the resulting thin topsides (see plate 6.3).

In method E, the hull is solid, but in two halves cut longitudinally and vertically. Each half is carved to the shape of the port or starboard side by the use of templets as already described for the solid hulls; and then a thin plank of wood, cut to the shape of the stem, keel and sternpost viewed in elevation, is glued between the two halves, as on a 74 gun ship model in Peterborough museum.

These are the basic methods, and I will now go on to describe the variations to be found; some features of one method often being incorporated in another method. Some of those made with solid hulls are left plain, with the wood either varnished, polished or painted to represent copper,[14] the black wales between the lines of gun ports being painted on. Others are sheathed up to the water line, as already mentioned, with copper. This may be strips of the metal nailed on, or sometimes the copper is cut into rectangular pieces, always over scale size, to represent the plating.[15] In a few exceptional cases the whole of the underwater body of the hull is covered with one piece of copper, moulded or beaten out to shape, examples of which may be seen in Peterborough museum and at Arlington Court and in plate 11.2; which obviously could be done only by a man familiar with the technique of sheet metal working. Some are to be seen in which the sheathing is not of copper sheet fixed in these ways, but paper-backed metal foil glued on to the hull. One small model in Liverpool museum of a three masted, lug sail, revenue cutter is sheathed with strips of straw, coloured green, and has an extraordinarily realistic appearance of weathered copper.

But whichever building method is adopted, in order to simulate the appearance of the real thing, the frames in a built-up model, or the

14
See plate 3.2

15
See plate 9.1

16
Compare the planking in
plates 6.5 and 6.8

17
See plate 6.8

hull in a solid model, it has to be covered with planking; this,
in the vast majority of the models, is of bone or wood, riveted or
nailed on. When the planks are of bone, they vary considerably in
width from model to model, with little or no regard to the scale of the
model,[16] but it would seem according to the measurements of the
material which happened to be available.[17] Very rarely are they carved
to fit but most often bent into place, and where they have been forced
into position, as opposed to having been fitted into place, cracks have
sometimes appeared in the course of time, and occasionally they have
sprung away from the solid core beneath.

6.4 An example of an otherwise workmanlike wooden model where the solid hull
has warped and split during its long life; perhaps one of the reasons why
comparatively few wooden models have survived

Note that here some details such as guns, anchor stock and gratings are rather
surprisingly made of bone. *Courtesy of Arthur R. Sawers, Chicago, U.S.A.*

The thickness also varies, but is usually about one thirty-second or one sixty-fourth of an inch, though where the surface has been smoothed off with abrasives it has reduced this still further. In the case of the large bone model in the Watermen's Hall, to be described later, the planking is about one-eighth of an inch thick and is fixed to frames. When the planking is of wood, the comparative ease with which this material can be worked has produced much better results, not only in the fact that the models are often truer to scale but also in the more realistic appearance of the finished article.

It is not an easy and straightforward task to fix the planks to a hull, but one requiring great care and the skill that comes with experience. For the surface of a hull is a complication of many convex and concave shapes, with the area to be covered amidships greater than that at the bow or stern; or in other words the girth at the midship frame is greater than that at the bow or stern. Consequently the planks must be wide at the middle and taper off towards the ends so that, there, the planks are slightly narrower; also they must be curved in order to lie to the side of the hull and so follow its contours. If the skin of a hull is developed on to a flat surface, it will be seen that the curves vary,

6.5 LE VENGEUR and 6.6 OCEAN   These photographs show examples from two different models of very expertly laid planking. It can be seen that in the bow view the planking tapers off to fit into the stem, and in the stern view the planking tapers up to the transom but widens out to fit into the rudder post. *6.5, The Science Museum, London. 6.6, Crown Copyright, The Science Museum, London*

some planks need to be almost in the shape of an arc of a circle, whilst others are the shape of an elongated S. Straight strips can never be made to fit accurately, they will buckle if forced into position.

Furthermore, if we follow the run of any strake along the side of the hull, it will be seen that it twists and turns as it passes from stem to stern. The garboard strake, that is, the plank nearest to the keel, for instance, is vertical at each end and almost horizontal at the middle. As for a plank at the bilge, this is vertical at the stem and then

6.7 Here can be seen in close-up the stern of another model showing butt joints in the planking which are not sufficiently staggered and do not join on a frame. Also there is a very wide taper to two of the planks coming to the rudder post and these are of course considerably over scale. Note also that in this model the rudder is not hinged as it is in the model shown in the previous photograph. Note also the painted wales, nailed-on gun port lids, and chains made incorrectly of twisted wire.
R. Creagh-Osborne

6.8 This model shows a very poor example of planking where the bone strakes are very haphazardly assembled with little regard for authenticity. *R. Creagh-Osborne*

gradually turns until it is very nearly horizontal as it runs beneath the counter, whilst a plank at the bulwarks is, practically speaking, vertical for its whole length. Thus, it is easy to see, much thought must go into the planking of a hull, and careful measurements made as the work proceeds. The dexterity displayed in many of the models could have been acquired only by continual practice, accompanied by a clear knowledge of what is entailed, and so cannot be said to be the work of a novice.

In the best specimens this planking is symmetrical; both sides of the hull bear the same number of strakes; each strake has its exact counterpart on the opposite side, all strakes are of the same width along a vertical line, the width being of a size to correspond with the scale of the model, and the joins of the butts of the planks are staggered, but are in vertical lines corresponding to the positions of the supposed frames.

There are examples of bone planking, however, where no attempt is made to balance one side with the other, neither to make the strakes of equal width, nor to place the butts of the planks in vertical lines, but only to fit the joints just as the material required. Thus this standard of work has a haphazard look, composed as it is of unequal sized pieces of bone, quite unlike the appearance of a full-size ship, and therefore obviously of inferior quality.

The stern and quarter galleries are frequently built up of pieces, each part being riveted in place and accurately fitted so that the carved decoration is not affected but merges from one piece to the next. This

6.9 This is a typical horse-shoe shape of stern with British trophies carved upon it. The stern is made in three parts and measures three and three-quarter inches wide. The quarter galleries measure one and three-eighth inches wide and one and seven-eighth inches high. Superb examples of stern and quarter galleries can be seen in photographs in this work particularly in plates 7.5, 8.3 and 8.9. *A. Ebelthite, Author's collection*

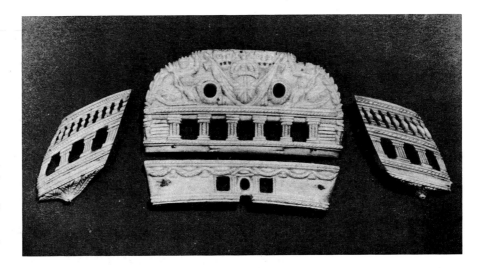

is accomplished by mounting the unfinished pieces of bone, previously cut to size and shape, on a suitable temporary base, in the relative positions they will eventually occupy. The various figures, balustrades, decorations and lights are then carved, the whole thing subsequently taken apart and then refixed in its permanent position on the model.

Figureheads

The figureheads were similarly constructed and if very small are carved from one piece of wood, bone or ivory. The larger ones are built up by the method of riveting arms and legs to a body, and then adding a sword, shield, wreath, palm, torch, distaff or some other motif in keeping with the name of the vessel.

This technique was necessary because, as we have seen, only small pieces of suitable bone could be obtained. But the joints are so accurately fitted that frequently it is only where a joint has opened, or the material has twisted or distorted, that it has become visible; otherwise it is only by careful search that the joint can be discovered.

Decks

The decks are either built *in situ*, but more usually rabbeted in, or rested on supports as a separate unit, and if this is so, can be lifted out completely with all the deck fittings.[18] In a bone model, the deck is a piece of wood, planed on one side but often rough on the underside, covered over with thin bone strips to represent the planking. Sometimes these strips are all of the same width, and in the best examples are of a scale size, but in others according as the material available fitted. Consequently if the deck planks are of different widths, they give an unbalanced and jumbled effect and do not look

18
See plate 6.14

so neat as an evenly laid deck with nice straight lines.

In Arlington Court is an unfinished bone model of a ship, and as such provides a very interesting study for here we can see the intermediate stage in the construction of a model. The hull is completely finished and the deck is ready with all deck fittings for the erection of the masts and rigging, certain items of which have already been fixed. This is

6.10

6.11

6.12

6.10, 6.11 and 6.12 Examples of figureheads. That shown in plate 6.10 is carved out of a solid piece of bone whereas the other two have arms made separately and added on afterwards. The example shown in 6.10 has an actual height of one and three-eighth inches and is painted in several colours. The figurehead in plate 6.11 comes from the model of the LE VENGEUR, a French 74 gun ship made in Portchester Castle by prisoners in 1798. The figurehead in plate 6.12 comes from a French 120 gun ship which apart from this item is entirely made of wood. *6.10, A Ebelthite. 6.11, The Science Museum, London, 6.12, Crown Copyright, The Science Museum, London*

the usual method adopted by the ship model maker, for before the masts and yards can be erected and the model rigged, the deck work must be completely finished, otherwise, when the model is rigged, to do any further work on the deck is exceedingly difficult, if not impossible, without damage either to the delicate rigging or to other parts of the model.[19]

19
See also plates 6.15, 6.16 and 9.1

The following photographs will serve to illustrate how the bone models were made, and perhaps help to clarify what has just been written. I am indebted to W. H. Honey Esq. for the photographs and for providing details of the model which he has restored to its very fine present condition. They show the various stages of the progress of the work on the model which is a flush-decked frigate of 46 guns bearing on its stern the name the GLORY. It is apparently to a scale of 1 : 150, the length of the gun deck being thirteen inches.

6.13 The flush-deck frigate of 46 guns, the GLORY, in a damaged state awaiting restoration. *W. H. Honey*

The first photograph shows the model in its damaged condition. Where a model is received in such a state, and provided all or most of the parts are still present, there is only one thing to do and that is to dismantle it completely, so as to be able to clean away the dirt and grime accumulated over the decades, but preserving as far as possible the original rigging. This Mr. Honey did, and the second photograph shows the hull of the model taken to pieces and the component parts laid out ready for reassembly.

Before proceeding further there are one or two things worth noticing about the parts as shown. The hull has dark wales which extend from stem to stern in one piece and are made of baleen, which is the material frequently used for this purpose. It is also worth noting the evenness of the planking and that the butt joints of the planks meet correctly on the vertical lines of the imaginary frames, and how they taper

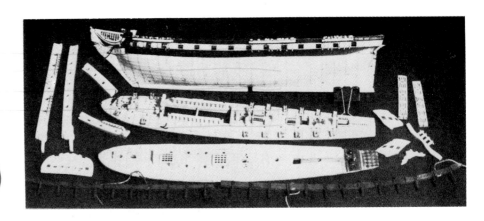

6.14 The same ship dismantled for restoration. The length of the hull is fifteen and a half inches. *W. H. Honey*

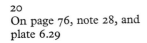

20
On page 76, note 28, and plate 6.29

towards each end. The top deck is fully planked, the planks being narrow and almost of scale size. The gun carriages are riveted to the deck and surrounding the open waist can be seen the carved balustrading. The gun deck is also fully planked and has two cabins aft, the floor of one of which is covered with chequer-board straw marquetry, of which I shall have more to say later.[20] At each side of the photograph are various fittings such as the stern and quarter galleries, and the parts which make up the bulwarks and hammock nettings; all this is of bone. In the foreground can be seen the curved wood strips carrying the dummy guns, which fit behind the gun ports in a special way I shall describe in detail in a later passage.

6.15 The deck is absolutely complete and all the fittings are in position. Only then can the rigging be started. Here the foremast and bowsprit are in position. *W. H. Honey*

6.16 All the lower masts are now rigged and the tops are fitted. *W. H. Honey*

The next photograph, taken from the port side, shows the model partly assembled, and the foremast erected with its shrouds and forestay, and the top fitted. In the next photograph, taken from the starboard side, is shown the three lower masts complete with their tops and standing rigging. The last photograph shows the model completely restored, fully rigged, the boats hanging from the yardarms and the stern davits, and placed in its glass case.

6.17 The GLORY complete and under its glass bell-jar. See overleaf for further close-up details. *W. H. Honey*

6.18   This detail photograph shows the port bow of the GLORY. Note the figure-head holding a wreath and with a separate arm riveted on, the carving on the trail board, the scarfed joint on the mast, the run of the hull planking, the well-finished anchor, the carving of the hammock netting, the nice boats and the anchor buoy hanging in the rigging. *W. H. Honey*

6.19   The starboard side of the GLORY. Note the rigging details and the fittings on deck, i.e. capstan, fife rail and pin rail. Also the skylights and the double-sided hammock netting. *W. H. Honey*

6.20   The foretop of the GLORY. Note the bone dead-eyes and lanyards, the crows
foot and euphroe block, the forestay and preventer with snaking in between, the triple
block hanging below the top, and the masts fished and woolded. *W. H. Honey*

In a similar photograph is seen another model dismantled for restoration. This is a 100 gun ship of three decks and here again the dark wales are of baleen, but notice that the hull planking is not so fine an example. The lines of rivets are not equally spaced nor are they in vertical straight lines. The butt joints of the planks meet between imaginary frames and so the appearance is not so good. The deck planking, however, is better, being of narrow planks evenly laid and so has a neater look. But notice the unfinished ends to the deck planking which will eventually be covered by the poop deck seen in the foreground. Though this will not detract from its appearance when finished, it is typical of unseen parts which are so often left in a rough state. In this model also, the bulwarks are plain and the hammock nettings are stanchions and rope lines where usually, as in the previous model, is found perforated and carved bone work.

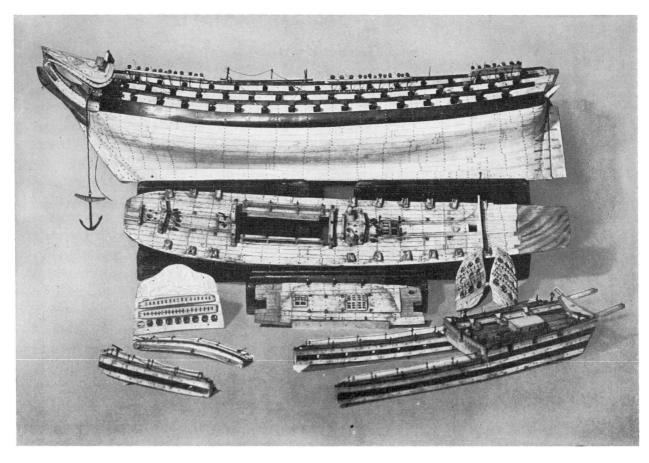

6.21 100 gun ship dismantled for restoration. Note the bone planking of the deck with unfinished ends. Also the butt joints of the hull planking which in some cases are between the frames. The dark wales are made of baleen. *W. H. Honey*

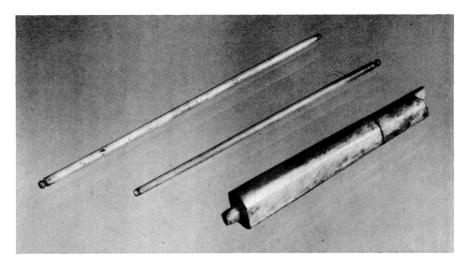

The masts and yards (which in the best specimens are correctly tapered) are built up to the required length, if of bone, with short pieces scarfed or half-lapped together. The joints are through riveted with iron, brass or copper wire and are often hidden by metal mast bands, or by woolding of cotton, thread, paper or metal foil. The topmasts are often fidded, and the yards frequently rigged with studding sail booms. The tops, trestle trees and crosstrees are all built up of small pieces of bone riveted together.[21]

The masts themselves are occasionally stepped through the deck and for some distance into the solid core, or down to the keel in a built-up model, and so stand rigid; but more often than not the method is for the masts to have short tenons at their bases, which fit into mortices in the deck.[22] They are then supported only by the rigging, consequently if the model is damaged, and it is usually the rigging which suffers most, a mast may lose its support and fall. In doing so the rest of the rigging is damaged and the other masts as well become loose. The restorer of the model is then faced with quite a problem to disentangle the broken rigging from the masts and spars.[23]

The rigging itself is sometimes of hair, usually of course only in the smaller models, but in the bigger models is made up of cotton or thread in exactly the same way that real rope is made. Without going into the technique of making model rope, which is practised by the best model makers, and is fully described by the author in the January 1959 issue of *Model Maker*, it should be said that rope is laid either clockwise or anti-clockwise, i.e. right-handed or left-handed.[24] Most ropes in a ship were three-stranded and right-handed of various

21
See also plates 5.3, 5.4 and 6.18

22
See plates 5.3, 5.4 and 6.22

23
See plates 6.13 and 8.4

24
See plates 5.11 and 5.12

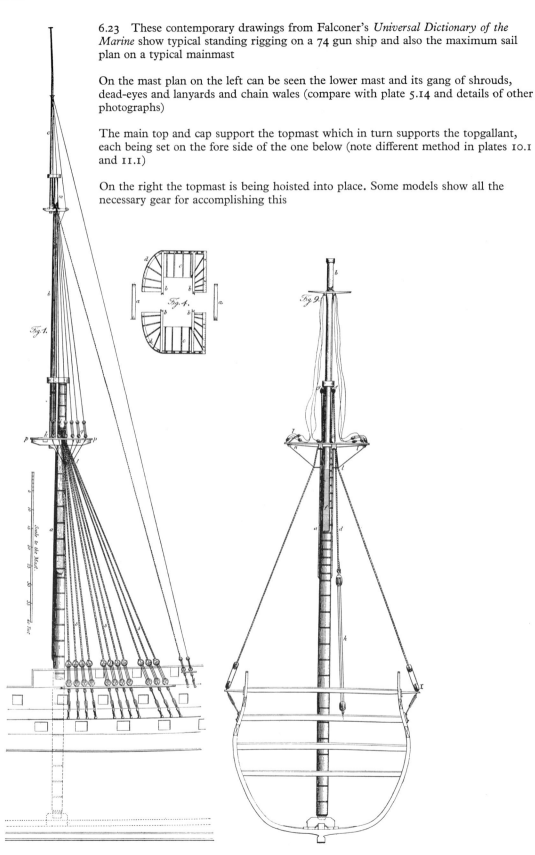

6.23 These contemporary drawings from Falconer's *Universal Dictionary of the Marine* show typical standing rigging on a 74 gun ship and also the maximum sail plan on a typical mainmast

On the mast plan on the left can be seen the lower mast and its gang of shrouds, dead-eyes and lanyards and chain wales (compare with plate 5.14 and details of other photographs)

The main top and cap support the topmast which in turn supports the topgallant, each being set on the fore side of the one below (note different method in plates 10.1 and 11.1)

On the right the topmast is being hoisted into place. Some models show all the necessary gear for accomplishing this

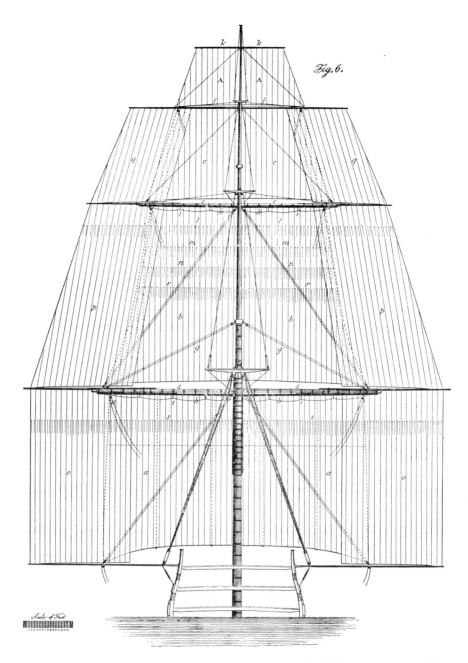

6.24 The sail plan shows at the top a royal mast and sail which were not normally set, though some models show them. Also the maximum number of studding sails (*coll.*: stuns'ls) and their booms, again shown on many models but seldom all used in practice (see plate 6.22 for a detail of studding sail booms)

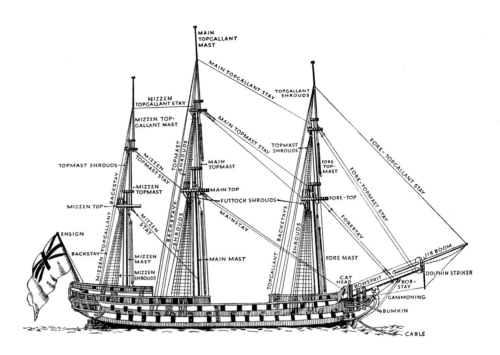

thicknesses, but the shrouds were made of four-stranded, left-handed rope,[25] and the anchor cables also were left-handed, but three-stranded. In the best models this is reproduced as on a real ship and clearly demonstrates the fact that the makers were practical seamen and knew their profession, if one can so call it. The rigging is correctly rove off, and so carefully and accurately is this done, that in the most superior of the models, if necessary, the yards could be raised and lowered and the ropes worked as in a real ship, if only the sailors were Lilliputians.[26]

6.25 This photograph shows three-stranded left-hand-laid anchor cable. Note that this anchor is made out of flat sheet metal and twisted. A very poor representation and not comparable with the quality of the rest of this particular model. Note the anchors in plates 6.18, 6.21, 12.1 and the Frontispiece.
R. Creagh-Osborne

25
See plates 5.13 and 5.14
26
See rigging details in plates 5.11–5.14, 6.18–6.20 and 6.23, 6.24

Many fascinating elaborations may be noted in the prisoner models, one of the most attractive being that the guns can sometimes be run in and out by pulling on a cord or cords emerging from the bow or stern, or occasionally from the base through the keel. The mechanism

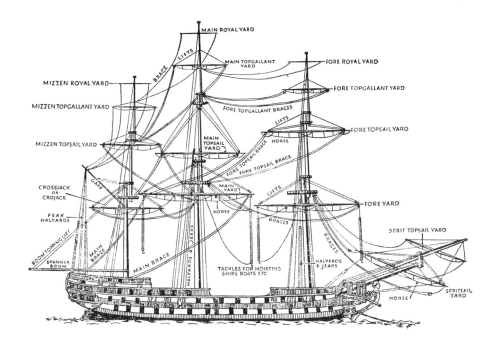

6.26 and 6.27 Two draw-
ings from C. Northcote
Parkinson's book *Portsmouth
Point* which are helpful in
identifying standing rigging
(6.26) and running rigging
(6.27), reproduced with the
permission of the *University
Press of Liverpool*

*Gun retracting
mechanism*

27
See plate 6.3

for this operation is really quite simple and reference to the illustra-
tions will make it clear. In the photograph of the interior of the
GLORY,[27] note first the way in which the model has been made. A
solid block of wood has been carved to shape and the interior hollowed
out down to the gun deck leaving the thin hull sides out of which the
gun ports have been cut. The pulling cord for operating the guns
comes up from the keel through the hole seen amidships, it then
divides in two going forward and aft over the bone fairleads seen
each side of the hole, over the rollers which are hessian wrapped
round bone, and then each divides again in two, and the ends are
attached to the gun planks, which are the strips of wood carrying the
dummy guns seen in plate 6.14, foreground. These are held apart by
transverse springs and so, when the cord is pulled, the guns are
drawn back into their ports and disappear, when the cord is released
the guns emerge from their ports by the pressure of the transverse
springs.

In the 100 gun ship the mechanism is intact, but in this case the pulling
cord emerges from the stern. It can be seen that it runs through holes
cut in blocks of wood fixed to the core of the hull, that it divides fore
and aft and is attached to the gun planks, which are kept apart by the
transverse springs which are also visible. Sometimes the pulling cord
emerges from the bow at the hawse holes, but this is not a usual
method.

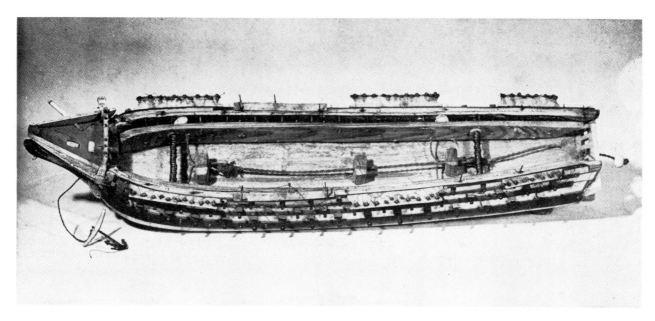

6.28   The interior of the 100 gun ship showing gun retracting mechanism. The guns are fixed to the two curved longitudinals mounted just inside the ship's side. They are pushed outwards against the ship's side by the coil springs fore and aft. The twisted rope connected to the longitudinals in two places runs via fairleads and out through the stern and has a bone knob on the end. A pull on this will retract the guns

Plate 6.3 shows another hull with fairleads arranged for the operating cord to emerge centrally from the keel. *W. H. Honey*

Naturally after such a long time the springs have broken or rusted away in many of the models and so the mechanism does not work. Unfortunately unless the model is completely dismantled so that the deck can be removed, it is impossible to put the gun retracting gear into working order again, since it is necessary to get at the space between the gun planks, as the photographs show.

Referring again to the GLORY and the compartments at the stern of the gun deck, the aft compartment is covered with inlaid straw marquetry of a chequer-board design,[28] which design was the one usually used on the canvas or oil-cloth which covered the floor of the captain's cabin in the real ships of the time. Though the flooring can be picked out in the photograph, what is not so clear is the fore compartment in which two officers made of bone, and coloured to represent them dressed in their uniforms, are seated at a table on which is a carafe of wine and two tumblers. These can be seen in the finished model only by looking through the stern gallery windows which are made to open, but plate 6.29 shows the scene during restoration of the model and before the gun deck was replaced. The photography is not too good owing to the small size of the figures and

6.29   The interior of the after cabin of the GLORY showing figures seated at a table with wine and tumblers in front of them.
W. H. Honey

28
Just visible in plate 6.14

the difficulty of focusing; but as shown, the figures are approximately actual size.

Only very occasionally are the models equipped with sails, and then usually only on those of the smaller sizes. They are made of paper, of cotton or of silk materials, now much discoloured and fragile because of their age. The reef points are either made of short ends of cotton or pencilled on in imitation. But in Arlington Court is a large bone model, fourteen inches long in which the sails also are made of bone.[29] These were obviously made from shoulder-blade bones in order to obtain the required size. They were then scraped down to make them very thin and thus almost translucent, softened by soaking in either dilute sulphuric acid or aromatic vinegar, and then moulded by hand, or with a burnishing tool so that they appear as if being blown by the wind.

BONE SAILS

Many of the miniature models, on the other hand, are shown with sails of extremely thin ivory that is almost transparent,[30] and this is fairly frequent, but sometimes the sails are made of some other substances that have the sheen and transparency of mother-of-pearl. I was told by a restorer of a few of these miniatures that the sails are made of thin flakes from the inner surfaces of oyster and similar shells; and certainly some of them look like this. It was also suggested to me that they might have been made from the thin flat membranes that are found inside the large claws of crabs and lobsters. But I have also been assured that some of the transparent sails are made from cow horns. The procedure was first to boil the horns to make them soft and then it was found that the layers of which the horns are composed can be peeled off. After this, the layers were carefully selected and the best beaten out in the manner of the gold beaters between folds of chamois leather, and then moulded to shape, cut to size and fitted whilst still flexible. But I must admit that I cannot say definitely which of these ideas are correct, perhaps there are examples which fit each suggestion.

HORN SAILS

However, the majority of these extraordinary miniature models are shown with the sails made of wood shavings of box, lime, pear or pine, which has mellowed with age to a warmer tint, almost the colour of mahogany; which has led to the statement often repeated, that the sails are made of this timber. But if careful examination is made of them it will be apparent that there is no pronounced grain showing, which leads me to suspect that lime and pear are the two most likely woods that were used. If a plane iron is sharp and set very fine, the

Wooden sails

29
See description on pages 105 and 106, note 59 and plate 6.30

30
An example can be seen in the Science Museum, London, and in plate 7.8

6.30 A bone model, fourteen inches long, of a 90 gun ship which has sails also made of bone and these show reef points and seaming. On deck can be distinguished some of the silhouette figures of sailors and on the stem the figurehead of a man in a top-hat. This is a very fine model and it is worth noting how beautifully regular the hull planking is laid and nailed to the frames, and the symmetry of the head rails and quarter gallery. A fuller description is given on pages 105 and 106. *The National Trust Museum, Arlington Court*

shaving comes out of the throat of the plane in a beautiful curl, just right for a piece to be cut from it, of the size and shape of the sail which has only to be glued to the yard.

Even the rigging in some of these tiny models is also made of wood; this may seem incredible but it is nevertheless true, that in many cases the ropes, as thin as a silk thread, are really made of wood.

6.31 Miniature model of a 74 gun ship, made entirely of boxwood. The sails are wood shavings and the rigging is also of wood. The hull of the ship measures about two inches long. Compare with plates 3.4, 12.6 and 12.7. *The City of Liverpool Museum*

Methods of making straw marquetry

The straw marquetry with which the ships themselves, the base-boards or the cases are sometimes decorated, was made from straight lengths of straw. The straws were split lengthwise, flattened, polished and dyed or coloured to the particular shade desired. The strips were then stuck side by side to large sheets of thin card or paper, each sheet being of one colour or tint. When dry and set, suitable pieces were cut from the sheet and fitted to pieces from other sheets of different colours, and a design or picture built up after the manner of a jig-saw puzzle. The resulting designs take the form of geometrical patterns or symmetrical borders and such like, but where the designs are very small, as in the central panel of a larger border and take the form of trophies of war, crossed flags, heraldic shields, motifs taken from the arts, stylized flowers or intricate intertwining branches and leaves, single coloured straws are glued individually to the background. Incidentally the straw marquetry designs were made up into baskets and work boxes and similar articles, and sold by itinerant pedlars in the Dunstable district from about 1800 onwards.[31]

31
See plates 2.2 and 2.4

Baseboards and supports

The ship models are supported on the baseboards in many ways: by the simple means of two chocks cut to the shape of the lower part of the hull and so forming a cradle,[32] or else by tenons projecting from the keel, through a mortice in the baseboard and secured by a tapered cotter as in the bone model named FOUDROYANT in the National Maritime Museum. In a few cases the tenon is a bone rod on which has been cut a thread and on to which has been screwed a nut, also of bone, and usually square. For additional support, threads of cotton are sometimes found running from any suitable place on the bulwarks, to small eye-bolts on the baseboard.[33] This is particularly the case in the miniature models, but the threads are, in these instances, often so fine that they are practically invisible, to such an extent that it is only if one is looking for them that they can be seen. This is so when the sails are held out to appear as if blown by the wind, for then an exceedingly fine hair is fixed from the sail to some point on the baseboard and merges with the surroundings.

32
See plates 5.8, 8.3 and 8.9

33
See plates 6.33, 10.1 and 12.7

As is very evident, much care has gone into the making of the models, but, curiously enough, the interiors and wood parts not usually seen are very often extremely rough. We can see tool marks not erased, and the interior of a solid hull crudely hacked out. Deck ends that are usually covered and hidden by the forecastle deck or poop deck, are sometimes sawn through only half-way and then broken off, displaying the fibres of the wood.[34] The deck may be beautifully finished, yet frequently the underside is left rough, with little attempt at careful fitting, quite out of keeping with the exterior appearance. The same applies to the baseboards which are often beautifully decorated with inlaid woods or bone, or straw marquetry, yet underneath have a rough surface just as the timber left the saw. Whether relatively unskilled labour was used to make up parts for the expert to finish off is a matter for conjecture, but nevertheless a likely possibility, seeing,

34
See plate 6.21

6.32 A fine bone model which is supported on two bone pillars on a base which is covered on the sides and top with straw marquetry. Note also the Victorian glass dome which protects the model from dust. *Courtesy of Arthur R. Sawers, Chicago, U.S.A.*

as I have shown, that frequently several men combined to make one model and the expert would hardly spend his valuable time on parts which could very easily be made by unskilled hands. But whatever the reason for this peculiarity, the finished appearance of the models belies the hours of toil that have gone into the making of them, the tedious repetition in making dozens of guns, blocks and dead-eyes, and the care needed in the complicated rigging of a ship of the line. However, having described the way in which the models are made, I will now go on to examine them further and in greater detail.

6.33 A very fine model of a French 120 gun ship in wood with solid hull, wooden lower mast and bowsprit, but bone topmasts, bone jibboom and hammock nettings. Note the delicate straw marquetry baseboard and the cord protruding from the stern for operating the gun retracting mechanism, and also the excellent launch and cutter. The model is supported on two small chocks. *Crown Copyright, The Science Museum, London*

Chapter 7

The ship models made by the prisoners of war, contrary to popular idea, are not rare. There are literally hundreds of them, and they are to be seen in most museums, sometimes in the historic houses of England, or in those which come under the care of the National Trust and are on view to the public, whilst a large number have found their way to the United States. Occasionally they are to be found in the shops of antiques dealers and not infrequently they are offered for sale amongst the *objets d'art* at auction sales, not only in London but also in the provinces by firms specializing in military and naval artefacts. Sometimes they may be seen amongst the contents of houses being auctioned, and occasionally they are advertised for sale privately. Even the suburban junk shop has yielded a bargain for a few shillings, to a knowledgeable and keen searcher. Unfortunately many have suffered damage during the years that have passed, either through age and neglect or spoiled to some degree through unskilled restoration.

Nationalities of makers   Though they are frequently and usually described or referred to as French prisoner of war ship models, there is no reason whatever to assume that the French were the sole makers of them. For we find in the lists of prisoners in the official registers of the prisons that men from many nations apart from the French were represented, including Italians, Swiss, Poles, Saxons, Spaniards, Dutchmen and, of course,

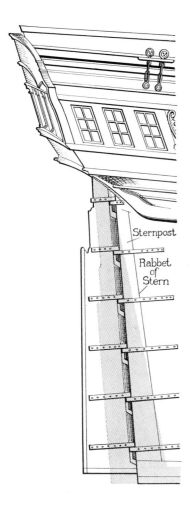

7.1 Typical examples of tracings from British and French sterns superimposed on each other. The detailed tracing is from the French ship AIGLE, 1782–1798, 46 guns. The outline shaded on top is from the British ship DUNKIRK, 1750–1792, 60 guns

Sternpost

Rabbet of Stern

7.2 A typical French sternpost with little rake. This is clearly shown in plate 6.14 where the rudder has been removed and may be compared with plate 11.2 of an English sternpost. *R. Creagh-Osborne*

Americans. But as the French were in the majority as regards numbers, it is only logical to conclude that they were therefore the more likely to have been the makers of most of them. Furthermore, the models bear the stamp of French influence by reason of the frequent use of the Tricolour, French ornaments, decorations and hatchments, French names after French ships and most important of all French characteristics in the details of rigging and construction.

But though the difference between French and British ships at the close of the wars was less marked, even at the beginning of the period with which we are concerned, the difference was only in detail. It is obvious that as improvements in ship-building were made, those features would be copied by other ship-builders, and when ships were captured during the Napoleonic wars, it was the usual custom to examine them closely, take off the lines and, if they were particularly good sailers, build a ship to the draught. The ENDYMION, a 40 gun frigate of 1797, was built to a design based on a French prize, LA POMONE of 44 guns. This latter vessel had low forecastle bulwarks which were not to be seen in English ships at that time, yet by 1813 had been generally adopted as an improvement in design, for the reason that it gave some protection to the decks against gunfire. Another difference was in the rake of the stem and sternpost, which in French ships was more upright than in English ships. The shape of the under-water body of the hulls also differed in that, as the French ships had a greater rise of floor and a sharper narrowing line, the cross-section of the hull amidships at the keel of a French ship tended towards a V shape whereas the English ships were more of a U shape. Apart from minor differences in the run of the rigging and the way the yards were braced, more noticeable was the comparative absence of sheer in the French ships,[35] the shape of the caps which were more square, the lack of quarter-deck guns beneath the poop, the typical stern which was half-moon or horseshoe shaped as in plate 7.5, and that of the OCEAN in plate 8.9, the curved ends to the light

35
See plate 7.11, Vaisseau à deux ponts

7.3 The mizzen cap and mizzen topmast crosstrees on a French-rigged model. *R. Creagh-Osborne*

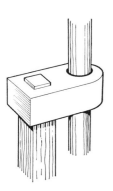

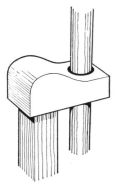

7.4 It was only at the beginning of the period under discussion that the difference in the shape of the caps was apparent. English above, French below

Characteristics of French ships

36
See also plates 3.2, 6.15, 8.1
and 9.1

37
See frontispiece

38
See plates 6.10 and 6.18

39
Cf. plate 10.5 of a Maltese
galley

side strakes,[36] and most noticeable of all the style of the figureheads which were more of a classical character such as Greek gods and goddesses, Greek warriors, Roman centurions,[37] female figures holding emblems of peace or war,[38] as well as kilted Scottish chieftains and other unusual carvings; but as I have said these differences tended to disappear as the years passed.

However, there are models that, as I have shown, were made by Americans at Forton; and there are others which bear Spanish or Dutch flags,[39] and are representations of ships of those nations, and are quite likely to have been made by seamen of the corresponding country. But in spite of this, which is undoubtedly true, I do not think I am far wrong when I say that it was the French prisoners of war who were the originators of the idea, and by whom the technique was developed, and that it was they who instructed the seamen of other nations in the art of making ship models of bone and other materials; so much so, that there are few European countries whose vessels are not shown in model form and which were made in English prisons. My reasons for this I shall give in the pages which follow, and show on what my belief is founded.

It has often been asked whether British sailors who had been taken prisoner by the French indulged in similar activities to those of their

7.5   A typical half-moon, or horse-shoe, shaped stern on a French model. This stern was not only carved but had a considerable amount of painting. The square holes under the stern galleries were for the gun-operating cords which, in this case, had broken off short internally.
R. Creagh-Osborne

86

confrères in occupying their enforced leisure time. But I must admit with regret that the British Tar appears to have been in no way so industrious, to anything like the same extent; but to have been more occupied in scheming to escape from the fortresses at Valenciennes, Verdun, Bitche and Givet where they were imprisoned, as described so vividly by Edward Boys, James Choyce and Captain O'Brien in their books (see Bibliography). The higher ranks on parole, in their way, seem to have associated with the English *détenus* of the towns, and to have made their lives as pleasurable as the circumstances allowed, for we can read of balls, gaming and even greyhound coursing as their pastimes. However, it must be said that the conditions in the French prisons differed greatly from those obtaining in England as the narratives of the prisoners show.

The only example I can cite of a model made by English prisoners is the one in Le Musée d'Art et d'Histoire in Geneva; it is a wood model of a frigate of 52 guns with three very tall masts and also a flying jibboom, which appear to be out of scale. The hull is carved from a solid block and strips of gold paper imitate the copper sheathing up to the water line, and the figurehead is a Scottish warrior armed with a sword and shield, but unlike those made in the English prisons this model is mounted on two quite plain wooden chocks. It was made by British prisoners of war at Toulon in 1807. Two photographs of

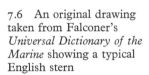

7.6 An original drawing taken from Falconer's *Universal Dictionary of the Marine* showing a typical English stern

this model may also be seen in *The Mariner's Mirror*, vol. 36, 1950, on page 153, and a short article on the matter may be read in *Marine Models*, vol. 6, 1934, page 260. See also plate 7.7.

Early models   Neither is it to be assumed that the bone and ivory models were a complete novelty of the Napoleonic era, for in Rosenburg Castle, Copenhagen, is an ivory ship model bearing the date 1634, that is, over one hundred and fifty years before the time of the Napoleonic wars, an illustration of which may be seen on page 146 of *The Sailing Ship* by R. C. Anderson, George G. Harrap & Co. Ltd.,1947, and it is inconceivable that in the interval no other bone or ivory models would have been made. Certainly a ship model was made by prisoners of war prior to 1759, for there is a large model of the FORMIDABLE of this date made by them that is now in Winchester College.

But it is indisputable that in the short period from about 1775 until about 1820 they reached their zenith of perfection, after which a decline set in, and that they finally disappeared about 1830. However, one sees the occasional model made by some amateur ship model maker in the tradition of the true prisoner of war model—a fine one of which, a 74 gun ship, I saw as recently as 1950, and a spritsail barge, the SALTCOTE BELLE, of which I have a record—or the crude and inferior fake passed off on some unsuspecting purchaser by a glib-tongued salesman. Since that time, however, a vestigial element has survived in the shape of small articles carved from ivory, including models of ships, which are made, or were made up to the 1930's, by workers at Dieppe, which town has been for two centuries at least, the centre of a trade in ivory carving.

Ivory models   From this town came the magnificent ivory ship model, LA VILLE DE DIEPPE, presented to Napoleon in 1811. It is now in Le Musée de la Marine in Paris and is of a ship of 88 guns, and on the base, as if rising from the sea (which is of inlaid ivory), are four horses harnessed by chains to the ship and being ridden by four cupids. There are also four other centaur-like creatures rising from the sea and blowing on conch shells. The ship is fully rigged with only the topsails set on the three masts, all the others being furled. The guns are run out from the sides of the hull and there is a profusion of carved detail at every conceivable place. Everything, I repeat everything, on this model is ivory, and that includes the rigging!

Many ship models have come from the ivory workers of Dieppe since Napoleonic times, and they are often described and sold as

7.7 This is the only known example of a ship model made by British prisoners of war during the Napoleonic wars. It is now in the *Musée d'Art et d'Histoire*, Geneva, Switzerland, who have kindly permitted its reproduction

First-Lieutenant Francis (known as Frank) Duval, born in Genoa but a naturalized Englishman, and his crew were captured after their vessel foundered. The crew were taken to Toulon, Duval to Verdun prison, but released on parole to stay with relatives in Genoa. The model was made by sailors of his crew during their captivity in 1807 and presented by them to Duval for whom they had a high regard

prisoner of war models, but this they most certainly are not. They are quite distinct and though they are models of small ships of the Napoleonic period, cannot be mistaken for the true prisoner of war model. I have seen many of them, and they are all of a similar pattern; so if I describe the one that was in my possession, it will not be excessively different from all the others which have been made since about 1830.

It is about three and a half inches long, the hull is made of a solid block of ivory and it carries fourteen guns. It is ship rigged, the sails being of translucent ivory and the rigging of ivory strands. Several tiny figures of officers and sailors stand about the deck, and certain details are picked out in red, such as the tompions of the guns and the insides of the boats, two of which are on the baseboard. The whole effect is one of fragility and has a fairylike quality, so delicate is the model. All the others I have seen are obviously of the same provenance and consist of models of 8 gun cutters, 10 gun and 12 gun brigs, 12 gun corvettes and other similar vessels.[40]

40
There is a fine example in the Science Museum, London, and see plate 7.8

Origins of the idea of bone models

I am certain that it was from the ancestors of these present-day ivory workers of Dieppe and West Africa, and from craftsmen of an allied and similar trade, the jet carvers of Brittany, who had been conscripted into Napoleon's army and navy, that we have the origins of the bone ship models made by the prisoners of war. As they had the skill and knowledge of working in ivory and jet, so they would have seen the potential of using pieces of bone as a substitute, and though it may have started merely as something to do, by whittling away at a piece of bone, it would soon have developed into a thriving business with profitable results. In this I am referring specifically to bone and ivory models, for ship models made of wood have been the hobby of sailors all over the world for centuries and the prisoner work was only a continuance of this urge.

Peculiarities of the models

But just as in primitive paintings and decorations we find a superfluity of detail so that every inch of space is covered, so too we find in these models that the largest and most complex variety of each class is more commonly represented, and not satisfied with that, the maker has added more guns than were normally carried so that nearly all the three-deck ships which usually had about 100 guns are shown with 120, and sometimes even more, the 74 gun two-deckers have at least 80, while the frigates usually armed with about 46 guns rarely have less than 50.

7.8. This 14 gun ship is made entirely of ivory, including sails and rigging. The hull is three and a half inches long and it was probably made at Dieppe after about 1830 and is therefore not a true prisoner of war model. *Courtesy of Arthur R. Sawers, Chicago, U.S.A.*

41
See plates 6.33, 8.1 and 9.1

42
See plates 3.1, 5.7, 9.1, 9.2 and 11.1
43
See plate 9.2
44
See plates 6.17 and 11.2

45
See plate 10.1

Many are shown with every conceivable fitting the maker has ever heard of or seen, whether authentic to the particular vessel, or whether applicable to the particular type of vessel or not. For example, studding-sail booms are frequently shown, not only on the foremast yards and mainmast yards but also on the mizenmast yards as well,[41] and on occasions even on the topgallant and royal yards, and spanker booms. These can scarcely have been practical when at sea, though the THETIS carried them in the 1820's on the mizenmast, but solely for the purpose of exercising the youngsters who had charge of that mast. We can also find fidded royal masts,[42] spritsail topgallant yards[43] and flying jibbooms[44] as well, which though neither unknown nor impracticable were extremely rare. It seems as if the makers thought that by adding all this detail they made their models that much more impressive.

Besides these larger vessels of war, many smaller and unusual types of craft are to be seen, from naval vessels to local merchant craft. To name only a few, we can see naval brigs[45] and brigantines, bomb

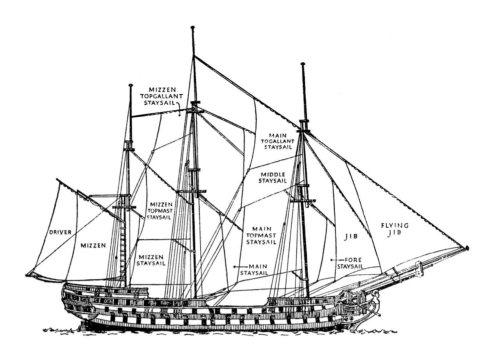

46
See plate 10.7
47
See plate 10.5
48
See plate 12.5

ketches, corvettes, and small lug-sailed Revenue cutters,[46] also craft of the Mediterranean such as Maltese galleys,[47] xebecs, fellucas, polaccas, scampavias and tartanes,[48] which shows that the makers must have had an intimate knowledge of, and be familiar with, these unusual types of vessels and not improbably be natives of the areas where they were usually to be found. For the range of these vessels was limited to such small parts of the Mediterranean Sea that only a person whose life had been spent along its shores could possibly have made models of them, seeing that the acquisition of plans of them was virtually an impossibility.

Scales of models No particular scale has been adopted for the models, and all ratios can be seen, from the one hundred feet to the inch scale of the smallest of the miniatures, up to the very largest scale of the bigger models. This shows the remarkable versatility of the makers in working in almost microscopic detail, or in the comparatively speaking easier larger scales. But it must not be taken for granted, that in the larger models more detail is to be seen, or that the miniatures are merely sketchy affairs, with only the prominent parts of the ship in evidence; for even in the tiniest of these, practically all details are reproduced with amazing fidelity. In fact, it is in the miniatures that one sees a most astounding display of craftsmanship. At scales of one hundred feet to the inch, a ratio of one to twelve hundred, gun ports will measure about one-fiftieth of an inch square, yet guns are shown pro-

MAIN TOPGALLANT STUDDING SAIL
MAIN TOPGALLANT ROYAL
MAIN TOPGALLANT STUDDING SAIL
FORE TOPGALLANT ROYAL
FORE TOPGALLANT STUDDING SAIL
MAIN TOPGALLANT SAIL
MIZZEN TOPGALLANT ROYAL
FORE TOPGALLANT SAIL
MIZZEN TOPGALLANT SAIL
MAIN TOPSAIL
FORE TOPSAIL STUDDING SAIL
MIZZEN TOPSAIL
MAIN TOPSAIL STUDDING SAIL
FORE TOPSAIL
MIZZEN
MAINSAIL OR MAIN COURSE
MAIN LOWER STUDDING SAIL
FORESAIL OR FORE COURSE
FORE LOWER STUDDING SAIL
SPRITSAIL TOPSAIL
SPRITSAIL

7.9 and 7.10 These two drawings will help to identify the fore and aft sails that might be carried by a three-masted ship and also the square sails. They are taken from the book *Portsmouth Point* by C. Northcote-Parkinson by permission of the *University of Liverpool*

49
See plates 6.30, 7.7 and 9.1

truding from them and the portlids of similar size are triced up; dead-eyes of even smaller sizes are drifted apart by lanyards so fine they can scarcely be seen, and on the deck skids[49] ships' launches and pinnaces are seen which measure about three-eighths of an inch long, but even these are shown with thwarts and oars in them!

Of course, many errors are to be found; for instance, we can see deck guns mounted directly behind the shrouds of the masts, in such a position that if they could be fired, the rigging would be shot away; an impossible situation no one can deny. Errors may be seen too as regards to scale; in some cases dead-eyes are as large as gun ports, which would make them about two or three feet in diameter, whereas they should not exceed about eighteen inches, which was the size of the largest dead-eyes in a first-rate ship such as the VICTORY; or the ladders have treads so far apart that only a giant could climb them, and gratings have holes often round instead of square and far too large. But these are mistakes of which one would only take notice if a highly critical attitude is adopted, or from a professional scale model maker's point of view.

Some details, too, are purely decorative, as for instance that on a model of a three-decker of 80 guns in Arlington Court. This has, extending along the whole length of the hull at the water line, a bone plank not only carved, but also pierced through to the inside of the hull which is hollow, in a lattice work pattern of leaves and roses, which of course is, from a practical point of view, just too ridiculous for words.

Anachronisms are also apparent, or is it a case of artistic imagery, when we see a full-hull model of a ship resting in two chocks or cradles that are fixed to a baseboard, but with a tiny sailing boat merrily scudding along in the foreground? Or when a rowing boat is shown manned by sailors pulling on the oars, towards a ship which is evidently standing on the surface of the sea? Or again, a ship with the gun ports open, the guns run out, all the sails set including the studding sails, the flags flying, but the model standing on a farm cart![50] Strangely enough, the ridiculousness of these situations is not appreciated until it is pointed out by a more worldly-minded observer. Surely a glowing tribute to the artistry of the anonymous craftsmen.

50
See plate 12.7

The vast majority of the models are shown with a full hull, and only occasionally can there be seen a water-line model, and then usually only in the scenic or panoramic models. There are a few, however, which combine both ideas and get the best of both worlds, and enable one to see the hull as it would be on the building blocks and also as it would appear afloat. This is done by placing, an inch or two above the baseboard, a secondary base which represents the surface of the sea and is painted or carved to resemble it. In this is cut a hole of the shape of the ship at the water-line. When the model is placed in position, it looks as if it is floating in the sea and an excellent idea is given of the appearance of the ship under sail, and at the same time the shape of the under-water body of the hull can be seen below the sea. The figureheads, to which I have already referred, are most frequently of an armed Roman or Grecian soldier, or of a kilted and helmeted figure with drawn sword. Female figures are also popular and they carry palms or wreaths, but I have seen one of a man in a frock-coat and top-hat![51] Another curiosity is that many of the figureheads are so similar, that it is a striking confirmation of the conclusion that one man would devote his talents to the carving of one particular item for others to assemble; in this case to carve the figureheads for several of the ships, and in fact it is noticeable that, on many models, the figureheads do not continue the curving flow of the stem, but seem to be just stuck on the bows of the ship and do not look as if they were really made for that particular model.

Similarity in figureheads

51
See plate 6.30

As an example, one type of figurehead of a kilted soldier, with a scarf or shawl flying in the breeze, is to be seen reproduced on many

7.11 This model of a 74 gun ship was made at Bishop's Waltham in 1812 and is now in Le Musée de la Marine in Paris. It is a full-hull model but is shown "floating" in a sea painted on wood above a secondary base. *Le Musée de la Marine, Paris*

52
See plates 8.1 and 9.1

models,[52] and though all are not necessarily the work of one man's hand, several of them appear to be so. Others, except for the objects held in the hand, whether a sword, spear or flaming torch, bear the imprint of one maker's work. Similarly, the female figures frequently strike the same attitudes, and bear similar characteristics in the carving, the differences being only in detail.

The baseboards are of many sorts and shapes, either square, rectangular, hexagonal or elliptical, and can be seen of plain polished

7.12 An example of a bone model mounted on a bone-planked oval base. *Courtesy of Arthur R. Sawers, Chicago, U.S.A.*

wood, plain bone planking laid like the deck of a ship, black and white chequer-board pattern also of bone, wood inlay of a geometrical or other pattern and straw marquetry of extremely complicated and beautiful designs. The baseboards are sometimes surrounded by balustrades of bone or wood,[53] the balusters of which may be round or square in section, and in either of these materials, or else fretted out of a thin flat strip. Occasionally swagged bone drapery surrounds the edges of the base and sometimes there is more than one base made by piling one platform on another as I shall describe later.

53
See also plates 3.1, 3.2, 8.1 and 8.9

7.13 An example of an oval base made in a chequer-board fashion. Note the shrouds are rigged through bull's eyes instead of dead-eyes which was the more usual method. *Courtesy of Christie & Co. Ltd., London*

7.14 An example of a model standing on a bone baseboard with a carved bone balustrade. *Courtesy of Christie & Co. Ltd., London*

7.15 This gives a good impression of the maze of rigging and the carving on the stern. The top armings also have carving, which does not show up in this picture. Though there should be two, the remaining cord hanging from the stern-chase port still operates the gun retracting mechanism. *From a private collection.*

7.16 This bone model about thirty-three inches long overall has been in the same family's ownership since it was bought from a prisoner in Portchester Castle. It has suffered some minor damage over the intervening years but the excellent rigging is original.

54
See plates 6.17 and 6.32
55
See plate 8.10 and also a similar case in plate 2.4

Most of the models have been encased since they were made, the greater number being merely bell-shaped glass covers that probably were formerly placed over clocks or wax fruits,[54] but some have the original cases which are as attractive as the models themselves, and consequently of greater monetary value. In Arlington Court,[55] two are shown with cases that have doors. The outsides of the cases are covered with a highly intricate herring-bone pattern of straw marquetry coloured in golden brown, blue, green and red. One of these cases is in the shape of an elongated hexagon and on opening the double doors, the ship is seen behind glass, but placed on the other five sides are mirrors, so that the model can be seen from six directions; either directly or by reflection thus: port and starboard broadside, port and starboard bow, port and starboard stern. A similar model is in the Victoria and Albert Museum in London, and can be seen on application, but plate 2.4 on page 21 of a model now in Chicago,

U.S.A., is practically identical in appearance with these models as well, and because of the similarities in them all, it is almost certain that whoever made one, made each of them.

It follows, then, that when it becomes necessary to analyse the models, we are faced with such a multitude of specimens of all sorts, sizes and materials, that many ways spring to one's mind how to classify them. But after due consideration of literally dozens of models, I think they fall most naturally into three groups, with sub-divisions to each, as follows:

1. Ships of bone, ivory, tortoiseshell or similar animal substances.
   A. Planked hulls.
   B. Solid hulls.

2. Ships of wood, straw or similar vegetable substances.
   A. Planked hulls.
   B. Solid hulls.
3. Scenic models and panoramas.
   A. Dockyard scenes.
   B. Harbour scenes.
   C. Miniatures.

Of these groups, the first is incomparably the largest, and of the various materials, those of bone the most common. This may be due to the lasting properties of bone, as opposed to the perishable nature of wood, which in the course of one hundred and fifty years and more has tended to become distorted, worm-eaten and warp and shrink if unseasoned,[56] and fall to pieces. On the other hand, it may be that the uniqueness of their appearance has disposed the purchasers of the bone models to preserve them, or even to the fact that their distinctiveness assured them of a ready sale when first made, and so were originally the more numerous.

Naturally there can be no hard and fast classification, for obviously there is much scope for overlapping.[57] The varieties are legion and no two models are exactly the same. Some models are made of both bone and wood, and there are others where it is purely a matter of opinion whether they should be described as a group of ships, or as a scenic model of a small convoy, or whether the miniatures should be listed under the materials of which they are made; though in this latter case they are really so distinctive that they automatically fall into a class of their own. But for the purposes of the descriptions of the most interesting of the models which now follows, the scheme I have suggested appears to be the least complicated.

56
Refer to example in plate 6.4

57
For example see plate 5.8 for a bone model with wooden stem, beak head and spars, also plate 6.33 for a wood model with bone upper masts, jibboom, hammock nettings and figurehead

Chapter 8

The bone, ivory and tortoiseshell models vary considerably in size, from tiny ships of less than two inches long, up to really huge vessels of five or six feet and more, but the majority are in the neighbourhood of between twelve and twenty-four inches long. Generally speaking, the smaller ones, up to about twelve inches, are the more interesting and fascinating, and seem to have the greatest appeal since one can take in the whole model at a glance and marvel at the dexterity so clearly displayed. Those up to about twenty-four inches long are the more elaborately carved and decorated, by reason, of course, of their being that much larger, which would facilitate the execution of finer detail.

The largest bone models

But as regards the still larger models, there is one called the HALSEWELL in the National Maritime Museum which measures about six feet long, and the guns of which are turned out of bone. This ship was an East Indiaman which was wrecked on the Dorsetshire coast in January 1786. Another large model about four feet long is in Rochester museum, and is of a three-deck ship carrying 132 guns made of brass, including the 26 on the top deck. The figurehead is of a man's head and shoulders and the hull has black baleen wales each side of which are rope mouldings made of bone.

There is, however, an enormous model in the Watermen's Hall in London, and it is alleged to be the largest in the world, with which statement I have no reason to disagree. It was made in 1825 by ex-prisoners of war, and was presented to the Company of Watermen and Lightermen in 1841, after having been won in a raffle for sixpence! It is a two-deck ship of 104 guns, and is about seven feet long and five feet six inches from keel to truck. The shrouds of the masts are set up to bulls-eyes instead of dead-eyes, which though an un-usual arrangement, was nevertheless authentic practice at this time in some cases. The decoration shows carved bone wreaths on the quarter galleries and window frames, and on the stern are carved two nymphs blowing horns, with a hart crowned between them. The figurehead is a soldier with a sword and shield, and other carving is to be seen on the rudder, with Maltese crosses carved inside the bulwarks. On the mainmast flies the Royal Standard of 1816–1837, which serves to date the model, but no name is to be seen, nor in fact can it be said to represent any particular vessel, and though it is a very fine model, I think it lacks the appeal of the smaller models; one can only stand amazed at its colossal size, and think of the venturesome spirits who made it.

Whalebone models   All these very large models appear to be made of whalebone in order to obtain the very long pieces necessary for the strakes, masts and yards without too many joins, and they are said to have been made by American prisoners of war, and though I have not been able to prove or disprove the statement, it has been repeated to me so often that there appears to be a tradition that this was their provenance. Certainly they are different in concept and workmanship from the other models, since there is a marked lack of intricate and delicate carving and decoration which is so noticeable a feature of the best of the smaller models.

It is in the models of twelve to twenty-four inches long that the carving, decoration and workmanship reaches its peak. In these the makers have let their imagination run riot, and their craftsmanship be given full rein. The skill displayed in carving such a material as animal bone in the way they have done leads me to believe that the sculptors were skilled craftsmen who were used to carving figures, flowers, birds, animals and heraldic or decorative designs in similar, if not the same, material of a hard texture such as ivory, jet, or jade, as well as precious metals.

As proof of this, in Edinburgh Castle can be seen four bone models of ships which it is known were made by conscripted ivory workers who came from Antwerp; and, as I have shown, Dieppe was a well-known centre of ivory craftsmen, and from West Africa, also, came exponents of carved work of the same material. Jet carving was a thriving industry in and around Brittany; and as for jewellers and watchmakers from Paris, they are world renowned in their craft, and, being familiar with the techniques of working in minute detail, would add their own contribution to the models being made, for from all these places Napoleon enlisted the men for his fighting forces.

That there were professional craftsmen amongst the prisoners is evident, not only to our visual sense, but also because we know that certain craftsmen of industries, unknown or unfamiliar in Great Britain, were given many concessions by the authorities. One French prisoner, by name Louis Felix Paris, was sent to London from Norman Cross on instructions of the Agent in charge at the depot because he was "an expert in the ormolu business"; for what purpose is not

8.1 Model of a 120 gun ship in bone on a baseboard of bone inlay. Note the French characteristics, i.e. upright sternpost and the curved forward end to the light side strakes. Also extreme features of prisoner of war models, i.e. fidded royal masts, a spritsail topgallant yard and studding sail booms on all three masts. The peculiar object hanging from the spanker boom is a form of lifebuoy or lifesaving apparatus. Compare the hammock nettings with the detailed photograph in plate 8.2. *The Science Museum, London*

stated but it may have been, and quite likely was, to instruct others in the secrets (as they then were) of the craft.

Another point to be noted is, that we can see exactly the same type of carving on several ships and which obviously came from the same hand. One distinctive strip pattern is a leaf and rose alternating,[58] and is used to decorate the wales or the edges of the bulwarks. Again, we find pierced bone of a lattice design that is exactly repeated on other ships. And, in two cases at least, the same pattern of horse head is used to finish the ends of the hances of the bulwarks. The figurehead with a scarf or cape flowing in the breeze I have already mentioned.

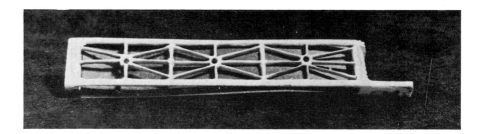

58
See Frontispiece on the beak head bulkhead. Also plate 8.9 on the drift rails

8.2   Hammock nettings made of bone. They were taken from a damaged prisoner of war ship model. Actual size two and three-quarter inches long. Compare with those on the model in plate 8.1 and also in plates 6.17, 6.18 and many other photographs in this work.
A. Ebelthite, Author's collection

To illustrate this point compare the photograph of part of a hammock netting, which came from a badly damaged bone model, with the same part in the photograph of the 120 gun bone ship model in plate 8.1, and you will see that they are of precisely the same pattern, and obviously the work of the same man. Or, for another more striking example, compare the stern of the OCEAN, 120 gun bone ship model in plate 8.9, with that of the HEROS, 74 guns (plate 8.3), which is in the Museum of Fine Arts, Boston, Massachusetts, and it is evident that except for the name, the one is almost the exact counterpart of the other in general outline, and when examination is made of the detail, as for instance the escutcheon on which the name is carved and the conch-blowing mermaids each side of it, the pillars supporting the stern walks and those on the balustrades, the figures and the horizontally carved grooves below the stern walk, the swags of flowers below the escutcheon and the similarity in several other details, it is quite clear that both these sterns were made by the same prisoner.

This does not mean, however, that all the carving on any one ship model was made by any one man, for often, as I shall show later, we can see on a ship model carving of quite different qualities. We can see the hand of the expert professional craftsman alongside the inferior endeavours of the aspiring apprentice. All this proves, without denial, not only that more than one man had a hand in the making of a model, but also that one man, skilled or with a flair in a particular direction, would make one item for inclusion in a model being constructed by the group of men, or would make, shall we say, figureheads, stern galleries, hammock nettings, guns, or any other part for the various groups of men making the models, to their orders and to the sizes required for a particular model.

There are still many fine examples of bone and ivory models to be seen preserved in England. One is at Arlington Court near Barnstaple, Devon, of an 88 gun two-deck ship made entirely of bone.[5]

59
See the photograph in plate 6.30

8.3 The beautifully carved stern of the HEROS, 74 guns, an exceedingly fine model. Compare with the stern of the OCEAN in plate 8.9. *The Museum of Fine Arts, Boston, U.S.A.*

It is about fourteen inches long and has bone sails, the guns also are of bone, and the planking of the hull displays splendid craftsmanship, for it is regular, symmetrical and exquisitely finished. It is flush-decked, that is without poop or forecastle deck, and on it stand flat silhouette figures of sailors made of bone. The stern galleries are carved, and attached to the rudder are chains also made of bone. The metal work such as the rudder pintles and gudgeons, mast bands and other fittings are of gold colour.

Also exhibited there is a three-deck ship of 136 guns, about twenty-two inches long. The figurehead is of a Roman soldier and is brightly coloured. The stern galleries are supported by beautifully carved nymphs, and behind the latticed windows is coloured paper. The stern bears Admiral's lights, and on the poop ladder stands the Admiral in uniform with cocked hat, while on the poop deck stand two officers also in cocked hats. One or two sailors are standing on the main deck, where also can be seen the pumps, ventilators and a capstan. But sitting astride the belfry is a pixie-like figure, which is so inferior in the quality of its carving, that it can definitely be said that this was made by another hand, and thus is further proof that more than one man contributed to the making of some of the models. Two boats are slung from the yardarms, and the gangways are lowered on the starboard side, as if the Admiral is preparing to leave by that side, for no entry port is shown on the port side.

In Trinity House is a model which bears on its stern the name FOUDROYANT. It is about twenty-four inches long, and has a wealth of carving seldom exceeded in other models. This carving is in bas relief as well as in the round, and has for a figurehead a kilted soldier with sword and shield. The stern shows four men supporting the galleries with upstretched arms, while below the taffrail, between a lion and a unicorn is a shield. All the other carving is in bas relief and shows the amazing felicity in working in bone and the inventive genius of the makers. On the trail boards Britannia in a chariot is being drawn along by birds. The bulwarks are plain outboard, but inboard are shown figures of animals and birds including a lion, a unicorn, several gulls and a man feeding a horse. On the top armings on the aft edge of the fighting tops are painted trophies of flags, and also placed there are tiny swivel guns. This is a model in which the guns can be made to run in and out by pulling on a cord which issues from the base, the baseboard itself being of inlaid bone and wood.

Another fine model is that of the TEMERAIRE in the Wool House

60
Close-up photographs of
details may also be seen in
Ship Models by C. Fox-
Smith, see Bibliography

Maritime Museum at Southampton, which has the merit of being of
quite good lines. It is thirty-three inches long and is planked on a
solid wood core up to the gun deck, and is planked on frames above
that with wide bone planks pierced for the gun ports. The tops and
yards are of wood, but the studding sail booms, masts and bowsprit
are of bone, which is unusual. This model has been restored, but is an
instance of restoration carried out carefully and with precision by an
expert, Mr. L. A. Pritchard, who has fully described the model and
given details of its restoration in the *Mariner's Mirror* for 1950,
pages 111–116, where also may be seen several photographs.[60]

8.4 and 8.5   These plates are of a bone model of a third-rate ASIA which was restored
by the author. They show the model before rerigging and after restoration. *Courtesy of
Sotheby & Co., London*

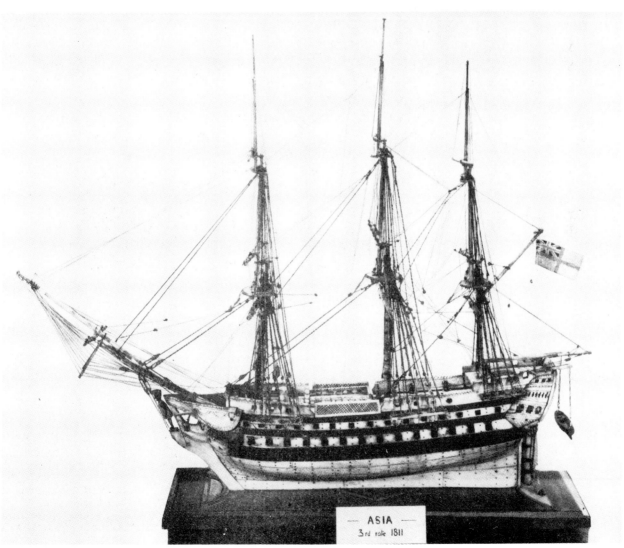

— ASIA —
3rd rate 1811

Though the TEMERAIRE was a 98 gun ship this model has two gun ports too many on each side of the three batteries of guns and the stern is typically French. The lines of the model, however, are not the same as that of the original draught which is in the National Maritime Museum and so cannot be said to be a true representation of the ship whose name it bears. On this matter I shall have more to say when considering the historical value of the models.

8.6   In this bone model note the curved ends to the light-coloured side strakes in the French style. The name is given as CONQUERANT (above the head rail). Note also the elaborate carved two-sided hammock netting.

The restored rigging is not to the same standard. Note for example the lack of preventer stays and snaking. *Courtesy of Christie & Co. Ltd., London*

But the most perfect specimen I have seen is that in the Eastgate House Museum at Rochester, Kent. Only twelve inches long, it is an exceedingly fine model of a French 74 gun ship. Though not elaborately carved, the workmanship is superb. The figurehead is a kilted soldier with a spear in the right hand, and his cape flying in the breeze. The dead-eyes are only one-eighth of an inch in diameter, but are pierced

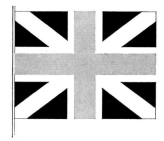

8.7 and 8.8   The drawings show the way the Union flag looked before 1801 and after. Below is a detail from a model showing a post-1801 Union flag. *The Parker Gallery, London*

with three holes each, for the lanyards. The blocks are about one thirty-second of an inch long and are drilled for the running rigging, which is made of hair, and could be worked to manoeuvre the yards. The euphroe blocks have holes one sixty-fourth of an inch apart, and the hair rigging forming the crowsfeet and running through them makes a mesh as fine as a spider's web. Studding sail booms are shown on all three masts. The hammock nettings, trail boards and fighting tops are of bone pierced to form an extremely fine network. The whole forming a model so satisfying and delightful that one can scarcely credit the label which says it was made "in the hulks at Chatham in 1795", though this was before the time the hulks were used for the criminal type of prisoner as I have shown. It "came into the possession of John Bullard, pilot and master of His Majesty's [George III] yacht CHATHAM". This provenance is fully authenticated by documents in the Guildhall at Rochester but the Union Flag on the forestay must be of later addition as it shows the flag which did not come into being until 1 January 1801; when or by whom it was added is unknown, but it was certainly there in 1900.

Tortoiseshell models are rare. There is one in Arlington Court, and is a small model of a frigate. It is planked on a solid core, which can be seen through the light transparent patches of the tortoiseshell. The base is of bone planks. Another one which I was fortunate to see and examine by courtesy of the owner is now in America, and I have been able to show her appearance by the photograph in plate 5.7. It is named the CERES, a sixth-rate of 18 guns, and is made to a scale of about one-eighth of an inch to a foot. It was reputed to have been made in Howard Street prison in Liverpool, and is said to have been commissioned by a Liverpool citizen about 1810. It will be seen that the hull planking is tortoiseshell but the remainder of the model is bone, and it will be noticed that the transparent patches of the hull planking give this type of model a characteristic appearance.

The solid hull bone models are also rare, and are usually small, for the reasons already stated. There are, however, quite a few solid hull models made not of bone but of ivory, the sails of which are made of ivory too, but thinned to such an extent that they are almost transparent. The rigging is also made of ivory threads, while the tiny figures of sailors sometimes seen on the decks are made of the same substance. They do not pretend to represent any particular ship, but only a type of vessel; even so they are attractive and delicate models and because of their size I have relegated most of them to the section on miniature ships.

Every bone model is different, there are no two exactly alike. Each one has points of interest which will repay careful inspection, for a whole chapter could be written on the carvings of the stern galleries alone. It is here that fantasy combined with reality and inventiveness with practicability are united so successfully. For instance, examine the stern of the 120 gun ship OCEAN. Notice the sixteen carved figures (did you count the two each side of the name?), twelve of them little boys and girls (or is it men and maidens?) discreetly hiding their nakedness with veils, and the other four, mermaids. To what are the two sirens at the taffrail listening? Is it to the music played by the two mermaids on their conch shells? Notice the difference in the thickness of the pillars supporting the stern walks. Massive at the bottom, medium thickness at the middle and light ones at the top. Look at the balustrades of the walks and admire the regularity of the carving and the delicacy of the twisted rope pattern. Notice the exotic flowers entwined with the central crowned shield, and the emblems of war and the trident of the sea god. See the leaf and rose alternating pattern in bas relief continued along the bulwarks, and the quarter galleries also receiving lavishly sculptured treatment. Then stand back and view the stern as a whole. How solidly satisfying it all is; how the designs flow one into the other. Now look below the stern carvings, and admire the beautiful run and fit of the planking, the metal pintles and gudgeons of the rudder, even the sternpost and heel has not been forgotten. Then consider the skill of the maker. Was he untutored? Never, that would be an impossibility. This model is made from common beef bones carefully saved from many meals, and could only have been the work of a master craftsman!

61
See Frontispiece

Now look at the figurehead of LE VENGEUR, a model of a French 74 gun ship made in Portchester Castle in 1798.[61] Admire the delicacy of the features adorned with whiskers, the plumed helmet, the tunic and the armoured kilt. How naturally the arms are poised even though they are fitted on separately. He seems to be waiting for a suitable moment to march forward! Wherever you look there is carving: on the ends of the boomkins, on the cat heads, on the bulkhead and the rails of the head. How beautifully the rails of the head sweep into the line of the bulkhead. Take note of the rigging, the anchor cable laid left-hand and secured to the anchor ring (which is served) by a clinch, and the ratlines correctly clovehitched. Then notice the running rigging laid as it should be, right-hand. The man

8.9 The truly magnificent stern with its ornamental carving on the model of the French 120 gun ship OCEAN. Compare this with the stern of the HEROS in plate 8.3. *Crown Copyright, The Science Museum, London*

who rigged this model was no ignoramus but a practising seaman!

In these two models alone is workmanship of the highest order. Is it small wonder, then, that they have been carefully preserved, and that they are a never ending source of enjoyment to those who love beautiful things and can admire the skill of a craftsman? But these two models are only representative of many others which may be seen in Britain and the United States, and in the next chapter I will list some of those that are of notable interest and say where they may be found.

8.10 A fine bone model with paper sails set in a splendid straw marquetry case with a drop-front glass door and internal mirrors. *The National Trust Museum, Arlington Court*

Chapter 9

The bone models and where they may be seen

Many museums have examples of bone ship models, some of which, it must be admitted, are not worth walking across the road to see, and some which are worth seeing are kept in store so that application has to be made in order to view them. This is a pity for though most museums have not the room to display all their treasures, it raises the question whether some do not realize the value of the models they might have; though let me hasten to add that I have found the greatest assistance in all the museums I have visited, a willingness to help me in my researches, and a readiness to show me whatever models they had, which at times was quite overwhelming.

Another thing I have noticed is that quite a number of them are damaged, which is understandable after all these years, but again it is a pity that where the damage is slight, and it is often not more than that, they are not restored, at least partially, for in a few cases this means only a little repair to some broken strands of the rigging, and a spot of glue to secure some fitting that has come adrift and which could be mislaid. To do this is quite a simple task, but if left further damage can ensue and it could then become a major overhaul.

On the other hand there are museums that obviously appreciate what they have and display them, as far as they are able, in suitable surroundings and do not relegate them to an odd, ill-lit corner where adequate examination is difficult. Though I cannot hope to catalogue all the bone ship models there are, nor would there be much point in so doing, a list of some of the most notable and interesting examples could prove of some use to anyone who wishes actually to see the models about which I have written, and for their own advantage get to know the difference in the types of ships, be able to compare a good model with one that is inferior, even to spot a fake, and see what makes one model superior to another. The following list is in no particular order so I will start in London.

Science Museum, South Kensington, London

This museum has reorganized its shipping galleries and in a well-lighted case can be seen two very fine examples of bone ships. One, the OCEAN of 120 guns, the stern of which is illustrated in plate 8.9, is extensively and elaborately carved, some idea of which this photograph will give. It is fairly large, the gun deck being about 24 inches long. The other model is also a 120 gun ship, but to a smaller scale, the gun deck measuring about 16 inches long. A curious feature of this model is that the figurehead, which appears to be a Roman soldier, stands with his arms outstretched sideways, and through his clenched fists run the jibboom guys.

Eastgate House Museum, Rochester, Kent

Here are to be seen two models, both of which I have described in the previous chapter. One, a large model 4 feet long, and the other, a smaller one 12 inches long, which is, I think, the finest bone ship model I have yet seen. This model should not be missed, and is worth going a long way to see, as my description cannot give an adequate idea of the beauty and quality of the workmanship.

National Maritime Museum, Greenwich

Seven bone models are in this museum, not all of which are on show. Apart from the HALSEWELL I have already described, there is another large model which is unique, it is of a Dutch brig, and though not very elegant is an interesting example and possibly made by ex-prisoners of war. A nice model 20 inches long overall, is called the MARECHAL NEY. The figurehead is a kilted soldier holding a baton in his right hand. The dyed bone wales have faded here and there to yellowish grey. The baseboard of another model of a first-rate about 9 inches long shows an interesting variation for it is inlaid in black, white and green coloured bone, and below the bow of the ship is a half-length, incised figure of Napoleon, and below the stern are two hearts pierced through by an arrow.

Worthing Museum and Art Gallery, Worthing, Sussex

Here is a small model of a 74 gun ship about 8 inches long, made at Dartmoor prison. It is on a bone baseboard and it will be noticed that the deck is made of one piece of bone, which is unusual considering the width necessary. It has been expertly restored but has suffered further slight damage.

9.1   A French 120 gun ship made mainly in wood. Note the correctly laid but over-scale copper sheathing and also the splendid collection of boats. Note also the characteristic French stern and the French style curved ends to the light-coloured side strakes. It also has fidded royal masts, studding sail booms on all the yards except the royals (even on the cross jack which did not normally carry a sail) and on the spanker boom. *Crown Copyright, The Science Museum, London*

Arlington Court, Barnstaple, Devon

This property comes under the protection of the National Trust, and has the largest collection of bone ship models to be seen anywhere, though it must be said the quality varies greatly, from one which I think is a fake to the extreme examples of four-deck ships, and also three-deck ships with 136 guns. However, the variety is enormous and every conceivable variation is to be seen: bone guns, bone sails, beaten copper hulls, copper plated hulls,[62] bone figures on the decks, bone chains and baseboards inlaid in wood, bone or straw. There are also some original cases, and a few have the names of the prisons

62
See plate 9.1

where they were made. Some of the models are of sufficiently high quality to have been displayed at international exhibitions, and in all there are about twenty bone models as well as four of ivory and one of tortoiseshell, so a visit to see this collection would not be a waste of time.

Peterborough Museum, The Priestgate, Peterborough
Here is the largest collection of work of every description done by the prisoners of war, and is well worth a visit to see the amazing variety of articles that were made by them, such as straw marquetry pictures, cut paper work, bone toys, bone clock cases and trays, and working models also made of bone. There are only about six bone ships there, but the whole collection will give an insight into the dexterity and inventiveness in the work of these prisoners who were imprisoned in the depot at Norman Cross, which is just a few miles away.

Watermen's Hall, 18 St. Mary at Hill, Billingsgate, London
Here is the largest bone ship model to be seen anywhere. It is about 7 feet long, and I have described it in the preceding chapter, but it is worth seeing if only because of its size.

Anne of Cleves' House, Southover, Lewes, Sussex
An extensively repaired model of a 90 gun ship can be seen here. It was made in Lewes gaol in 1815, but is not a particularly good model as it has suffered severe damage at some time and much of the original work is missing.

Trinity House, Tower Hill, London
A very fine model in bone of the FOUDROYANT, presented by John James Joass in November 1947, and which is in an excellent state of preservation. It has been described in the preceding chapter.

Royal Naval College, Dartmouth
This college possesses a beautiful model in bone of the BRITANNIA, of 120 guns, about 51 inches long. It is thought to have been made by ex-prisoners of war in 1818, and was purchased by public subscription in 1949 for £550 and presented to the college.

Wool House Maritime Museum, Southampton
The bone model of the TEMERAIRE to be seen in this museum is a superb model. I have described it in the previous chapter and given a history of its restoration. There is also a fine model of the frigate GLORY (not the same as the ship of the same name described earlier).

9.2 A French 40 gun frigate. Note the bone strakes of the hull without joins. A beautifully restrained model supposed to represent the English frigate AEOLUS of 32 guns, built in 1801, but all the details are characteristically French. Note also the extravagant fitting of royal masts and spritsail topgallant. *Crown Copyright, The Science Museum, London*

Royal Thames Yacht Club, Knightsbridge, London

In this club is a bone model of a 100 gun ship which is in very fine condition. It is illustrated on page 225 of the *Decorative Arts of the Mariner* (see Bibliography), and if this photograph is examined it will be seen that at the hair rails and round the waist are pieces of bone lattice work exactly like that I have referred to on page 104, obviously made by the same hand.

Royal Naval Museum, H.M. Dockyard, Portsmouth
This museum has recently acquired two very fine bone models and two others which may have been made by prisoners of war. All the exhibits are exceedingly well displayed and the museum is worth a visit in order to see other models of the Nelson–Napoleon period, for purposes of comparison.

Royal Scottish Museum, Edinburgh
In Edinburgh Castle some ivory workers from Antwerp were imprisoned, and the three bone models to be seen in this museum are reputed to have been made by them.

Glasgow Museum and Art Gallery, Glasgow, C.3
In this museum are thirteen bone models comprising frigates of 44 and 46 guns, and larger ships of two and three decks armed with from 74 guns up to 120 guns. There is also an 18 gun brig, which is an unusual subject for a bone model as they were mostly made to represent larger vessels. Another model is one larger than average of a 74 gun ship, and as I have remarked in a previous chapter in connection with very large models, this one is stated to have been made by American prisoners. The figurehead is of a man in a frock-coat. This is a very good representative collection.

Liverpool City Museum, Liverpool
Here is shown one bone model of a 74 gun ship.

Whitby Museum, Pannett Park, Whitby
In the museum of this seaport are to be seen representations of four bone models of 50, 64, 74 and 100 gun ships. This valuable collection is worthy of being better displayed.

Dover Corporation Museum, Ladywell, Dover
Here is an excellent bone model about 24 inches long, of a 74 gun ship with 6 carronades on the poop. It is called the CESAR, the figurehead being a Roman centurion, and has been exceedingly well restored. It is finished entirely in white bone, the hull strakes are nicely laid and the wales are edged with a rope moulding in bone. Though the model is not elaborately carved, what there is, is very finely done, especially the stern gallery, its surrounds and the quarter galleries. Two boats hang from the yardarms and one from the stern davits, all are fitted with thwarts and have oars lying on them. This model shows one of the extreme characteristics of prisoner models in that it has studding sail booms on all the nine yards, and a cord coming out of the side of the inlaid wood baseboard which serves to operate the gun retracting

9.3 This is a large model being fifty-three inches long overall, forty-three inches high. It is interesting to note it has the Royal Standard at the main (normally flown only when the Sovereign was aboard) and that it is the wrong way round. The Irish Harp should be nearest the mast and the Scottish Lion at the fly. The pattern of this and the other two flags date the model as after 1801. It is a very fine example and the rigging is in excellent condition and beautifully executed.

Other points to note are that the lower masts are fished and woolded, and that the fore topgallant mast has a scarfed joint just above the topgallant yard. Though the model is described in the catalogue as a British 110 gun ship, in spite of the flags and the Lion figurehead it has all the marks of a French built ship, i.e. the curved ends to the light side strakes (just visible behind the anchor suspended from the cathead), the vertical sternpost, the shape of the stem and the beakhead bulkhead. *The U.S. Naval Academy Museum, Annapolis, U.S.A.*

mechanism. This is a good model which appears to approach scale proportions, and is said to have been made by prisoners of war in Dover Castle after 1802, as the Union flag on the forestay is that of 1801.

Hastings Museum, High Street, Old Town, Hastings

Here is an attractive frigate in bone about 10 inches long, with a coloured figurehead, coloured armings in the tops, black and gold masts bands, and a nicely carved stern. The wales are of bone dyed black, which has faded, and the model is rigged with hair, and has a very long paying-off pendant flying at the main truck.

Woburn Abbey, Woburn, Bedfordshire

A very fine bone model in excellent condition of the NEPTUNE of 98 guns, which stands on an inlaid wood and bone base, can be seen here.

Museum of Fine Arts, Boston, Massachusetts, U.S.A.

Here is the bone model of the HEROS of 74 guns (plate 8.3), which is so like the OCEAN in the Science Museum (plate 8.9) that I suggest the two models were made by the same group of prisoners.

United States Naval Academy, Annapolis, Maryland, U.S.A.

This collection formed by Henry Huddleston Rogers has in it about ten examples of bone models amongst which are two models "floating" on a sea, one with a copper bottom and one with the bottom painted copper. They range between frigates of 40 guns and ships of 74, 100 and 128 guns. There are some very fine specimens in this collection. (See plates 5.15, 9.3, 12.1, 12.2 and 14.7.)

Other museums where bone ship models can be seen are Bristol City Museum, Queen's Road, Bristol; Pitt-Rivers Museum, Oxford; Maritime Museum, Buckler's Hard, Beaulieu; Chambers Institute Museum, Peebles; Orkney Natural History Museum, Stromness; and South Shields Museum, Ocean Road, South Shields; and I have little doubt that an enquiry at other museums will elicit further examples.

Chapter 10

The superiority of the wood models
Accuracy of scale and proportion
Carvel and clinker built models
Differences in types of models

The wood ships are superior to the bone and ivory models by reason of the fact that, not only are they more realistic as regards appearance, but also because of their being of better proportions, and closer to the originals in the accuracy of the details.

In the matter of the appearance, the fact of their being made of similar material to the original ships gives them a distinct advantage over the bone models. Furthermore, the amount of carving seen on the wood ships is less than on the bone models and the ideas are more restrained; consequently the model looks more like a real vessel and not a ship of fantasy.

Though, of course, a certain amount of the carved and gilded "gingerbread" work was still retained in the ships of the early 1800's, it was far less prolific than during the preceding century because of the acts of parliament prohibiting excessive decoration and because of the progress in naval architecture.

Accuracy of Scale and Proportion

In regard to the better proportions of the models, much of this may be due to the ease with which wood can be fashioned as opposed to the difficulties with bone, and also to the fact that large pieces of wood avoid the necessity for many joints, with their attendant difficulties and weaknesses, to make up the various parts of the ship. For instance, the masts or yards can each be made of one piece, and the planking of the hull which, as I have shown, is composed of curved strips, can more readily be cut out of a wide board and fitted with greater ease and more accuracy. For the same reason the material itself is capable of being worked to make fittings not only of finer detail, but also of correct scale.

Why the wood models should be better, in the ways I have just described, is not easy to understand, but it is certain that there are very few which are bad models; a statement which cannot be made in regard to the bone models, in which the quality varies enormously. Perhaps a reasonable explanation would lie in the suggestion that a rough, sailor-made model, such as is often seen gathering dust in a junk shop or on a market stall, and of which not much care would be taken, would have gradually deteriorated, become damaged and eventually been thrown away, but that a superior model, or one that was obviously of finer workmanship, would have attracted the eye of a knowledgeable person or that of a keen collector who saw in it something worthy of preservation. For it is a reasonable assumption that there must have been far more wood models made by the prisoners than have survived, because of the ease with which a model of something that looks like a ship can be made.

Carvel and clinker built models

There is another point to note, and that is that except for one solitary instance amongst the many examples I have seen, all the bone ships are carvel built; that is, the hull planking is fitted edge to edge so as to make up a smooth surface. But in the wood ships, not only do we find carvel-built hulls, but also clinker-built hulls; that is, each plank of the hull slightly overlaps the one next below it, in a similar fashion to the tiles on the roof of a house; a method of construction seen in rowing boats, in the small beach boats of East Anglia and in many other instances too numerous to mention.

Differences in types of models

Thus the range of types of vessels for the ship model maker who reproduces this kind of construction is immeasurably enlarged, and sure enough the prisoners have taken advantage of this fact; so that we find in the wood models, specimens, not only of large ships of the line from 120 gun ships down to 74's and 40 gun frigates which are of carvel construction, but also Revenue cutters, three-masted lateen-rigged galleys, Admiral's barges, Captain's gigs, small rowing boats and Maltese galleys which may be of the clinker method of construction, and all made as the prototype was made.

The two basic ways of building ship models, which I have described, are to be seen in most of these vessels: the built-up method and the solid hull method, and in the following brief descriptions, instances of these will be given.

A large model about thirty inches long of a 52 gun French frigate is in the National Maritime Museum. It is called the SIRÈNE, and is

10.1 A clinker-built brig of 14 guns. But note the fidded topgallant masts set abaft the topmasts, which is unusual but not unknown, also a stay wrongly fitted between the mast trucks. *The City of Liverpool Museum*

thought to have been made about 1823 by ex-prisoners of war. A built-up model, it is copper sheathed and has a bone figurehead of a mermaid or nereid holding a mirror, which motif is repeated carved below the taffrail. Small wooden figures are seen in various attitudes about the deck, and the sails are shown furled.

In the same museum can also be seen a 40 gun frigate about twelve inches long. This also is copper sheathed, and has a bone figurehead of a woman, brightly coloured in red and green, and holding in the extended right hand a wreath. This model shows one of the extreme characteristics of the prisoner of war models, for it has studding sail

10.2   A clinker-built three-masted lugsail gunboat. *The City of Liverpool Museum*

booms on the three lower yards of all three masts, and an extendable boom on the spanker boom for a ring-tail sail. The lower masts are wood, but the upper masts and jibboom are of bone.

There are details of another model described in the *Mariner's Mirror*, vol. 20, page 114. It is of a ship in a glass case with a painted background of Portsmouth Harbour. It is said to have been made by a prisoner in Portchester Castle, and represents an 80 gun ship. On the stern is the name MARS, it is sheathed with three horizontal strips of copper in a most accurate manner, and has much minute brass inlay work on the deck and bulwarks. It is also stated to be most beautiful in proportion of scale.

Of exquisite workmanship is the model of a 46 gun heavy frigate with poop of 1805, in the Science Museum. This is most beautifully made, the hull is superb, and shows the two-tiered quarter galleries and a stern with a projecting balcony. Six carronades on slides are shown on the poop. It is unrigged but carries the lower masts up to the caps. It may be unfinished, but on the other hand many models besides this prisoner of war model were frequently made in a similar fashion to this, and even so they make exceedingly satisfying models; this one being no exception. The model is both beautiful and delightful, and displays skill of the highest order, for the planking of the hull is both regular and symmetrical, with the pins fastening the planks to the frames giving it a most realistic appearance. The deck is laid in planks, with the deck fittings and guns accurately made. In fact, apart from the splendid workmanship, it is of such unusually good proportions that I should have thought it to have been made from drawings of the design, or at least by someone who had a knowledge of naval architecture and the construction and lines of ships of this type.

10.3   A heavy frigate with poop, 46 guns and 6 carronades. An extremely fine built-up model with superb workmanship both in respect of correctness of detail and scale proportions. *Crown Copyright, The Science Museum, London*

10.4 An example of an over-scale grating with incorrectly made round holes which were nevertheless easier for the modeller to make since they have only to be drilled. *R. Creagh-Osborne*

In Southsea Castle are two exceptionally fine wood models; one, LA GLOIRE, a frigate of 50 guns, is about eighteen inches long and is made of boxwood. The hull is built up and is planked in a very accurate fashion. The deck is laid in scale-size planks, the bulwarks are panelled and fitted with pin-rails and belaying pins. The rudder is worked by a double steering wheel and the rigging is very well done, the shrouds being set up to dead-eyes only one-eighth of an inch in diameter. The figurehead is made of ivory and is of a woman holding a wreath. It stands on a baseboard inlaid in a variety of woods of walnut, box and ebony, and also burrs of walnut.

The other model is larger, being about thirty inches long, and is of a 74 gun ship. What I noticed particularly about this model was the gratings on the deck and the one in the heads leading from the fore-castle up to the bowsprit. One of the most difficult parts to make, to anything approaching scale size on a model ship, are the gratings. They probably cause more heartburning and are more time consuming than many other parts, yet they are so often so shockingly made that when one comes across really good gratings, they are a joy to see. In this model they are excellent. In a real ship the holes in the gratings would be anything from about one and a half inches square to not more than three inches square, so that a man's heel would not get caught in them, and in this model the holes really are square and appear to be near scale size, so that they look right.[63] They are not, as is so often the case, round holes made with a drill, or roughly filed out holes that are supposed to be square, and which, if scaled up, would be large enough for a man to fall through! The rest of the model is of similar high standard and is in a case which, if not original, is of contemporary manufacture.

In Liverpool Museum is a built-up (planked on frames) model of a Maltese galley, ten inches long, which bears insignia of the Knights of Malta. It has three masts, each carrying lateen sails, and has thirteen oars aside, working on outriggers, with swivel guns for each oarsman. It shows the typical long beak and fighting castle, forward, and represents one of the last of the Maltese war galleys. The curved tilt over the stern is painted on the blue roof with a white Maltese cross, a portrait of Napoleon on the stern, and an angel below

63
See plates 5.10 and 10.4

10.5 A Maltese galley which is in the Science Museum, London, and, except for the decorative detail and the number of guns, is almost identical to that in the Liverpool Museum. The description of the latter on page 127 can apply to this model as well. *Crown Copyright, The Science Museum, London*

the stern overhang, and on the front of the canopy is a portrait of an infant. The shrouds are set up with tackles so that the lateen sail yards can be lowered and secured along the midship line.

A few of the wood models have part of the planking of the hull removed to show not only the frames but also part of the stores or cargo. A specimen of this type was to be seen in the Royal United Service Institution and was a frigate of 46 guns named LA FLORE. Below the gun deck, part of the outside planking had been removed and so the frames of the hull could be seen and, also, stacked in the hold, casks in which would have been stored the provisions for the crew, such as potatoes, flour, salt beef and other necessary items. Other models of this type are displayed in Liverpool Museum and the Science Museum, and demonstrate one of those lifelike touches often put in by the prisoners that lift the model out of the rut of being just another ship model and makes the study of them so interesting.

In the Science Museum are two of the clinker-built ships, one a schooner the other a cutter. These are clinker-built on frames and are to a scale of fifteen feet to one inch. The cutter is rigged in the normal way of the period and is armed with 12 guns, and has a portion of the hull planking removed to show the frames. The schooner is armed

10.6 A schooner of 16 guns. Clinker-built in wood it is flush-decked with two masts carrying gaff sails and square topsails. *The Science Museum, London*

10.7 A cutter of 12 guns. Clinker-built in wood and with part of the planking removed to show the frames. It is rigged in the normal fashion of the period but the gaff is shown in the lowered position. *The Science Museum, London*

with 16 guns, is flush decked and has two masts, both carrying in addition to gaff sails, square topsails. These two models are very detailed and executed in an extremely workmanlike fashion, and are beautifully proportioned.

Also in the Science Museum is a French 120 gun ship to a scale of twenty feet to the inch. It is inscribed with the name L'ARGUS on the stern and is very well proportioned and accurately rigged. One interesting point to note about this model is that it was made by French prisoners of war and presented by them to Elizabeth Fry, a pioneer of prison reform.

An unusual model is that in Liverpool Museum of a three-masted lugsail rigged Revenue cutter of 12 guns. The hull is planked on a solid core with straw of a green colour below the water line to represent copper sheathing, with natural colour straw above, and straw deck. Apart from the amazingly clever deception, only apparent on close examination, this shows in a vivid way the deftness and resource of the maker in using an unsuitable and unusual material with a most pleasing result.

Though the wood ships are not so spectacular as the bone models to the layman, to the ship model maker, whether amateur or professional, and to the person who is keenly interested in ship models, this class of prisoner of war models is probably the most rewarding from the point of view of authentic detail, and not least of all a revelation and a lesson in what can be achieved with inadequate resources and frustrating conditions.

Unfortunately, as I have already stated, they are less numerous than the bone ship models, but this does not mean that only those have survived which are described as prisoner of war models, for I am certain that some of the contemporary models to be seen in antique shops and museums were made by the prisoners. There are certain nuances, peculiarities and traditional treatment which inevitably stamp them as such, but the mere fact of their being made of wood has meant that their origin has been forgotten, and details of their maker been allowed to sink into oblivion.

Chapter 11

The wood models and where they may be seen

Though the wood model ships may not be so theatrical as those made of bone, they are probably of more interest to the ship model maker by reason of the fact that they show what can be done in uncongenial surroundings, adverse conditions and with inferior materials. They are also of historical interest in that they portray the enormous variety there was of sailing craft round the coasts, for the wood models range through the whole gamut of rigs of those days: sailing boats and row boats, and sailing ships which, alas, are not to be seen today. As regards the actual number of wood models, it is probable that there are not more of them than there are of bone models and the places where some of them can be seen now follow.

Science Museum, South Kensington, London

This museum has eight wood models in superb condition. They range from a galley to frigates and a 120 gun ship, and are well worth seeing, especially the heavy frigate illustrated on page 125, and the 120 gun ship presented to Elizabeth Fry—these two being particularly fine examples.

National Maritime Museum, Greenwich

Here are to be seen the SIRÈNE, reputed to be a prisoner of war model and very well made; two 40 gun frigates and also five charming boxwood models, none over 5 inches long, and all probably made by the same man. They have wood sails and wood rigging and comprise a cutter, two brigs, a frigate and a first-rate.

Liverpool City Museum, Liverpool

This museum has sixteen wood ships displaying a remarkable range of models. They comprise three frigates, each one different, a xebec, a brig, two 74 gun ships and a 100 gun ship, two gunboats, a cutter and a longboat, two 12 gun schooners and two luggers. The hull of one of the luggers is planked with straw to represent the copper plating and the deck is also laid in straw. Another model has part of the hull planking removed and shows casks stacked in the hold. The variety shown here from humble row boats, Mediterranean craft, coastal vessels to a 100 gun ship, makes evident the fact that the men who made these models came, not only from France, but from other European countries as well, and furthermore were familiar with the type of craft they have modelled in this collection.

Glasgow Museum and Art Gallery, Glasgow, C.3
An 88 gun ship can be seen here about 24 inches long. A very fine example, it is made of boxwood with much fine carving, and has a copper bottom.

Arlington Court, near Barnstaple, Devon
Nine wood models are here, amongst them an 80 gun three-decker that has a painted stern, with the name TRINCOMALEE on it. It is said to have been made by a French prisoner of war at Taunton in 1818. There is also a two-decker in which many of the fittings about the ship are of bone.

Southsea Castle, South Parade, Southsea, Hants
Two exceptionally fine wood models here should not be missed. They are a 50 gun frigate and a 74 gun ship, the workmanship is superb and amongst the finest examples of prisoner wood models. I have briefly described them in the preceding chapter.

Le Musée de la Marine, Palais de Chaillot, Paris
In the museum is a wood model of a 74 gun ship, and is an example of a full-hull model "floating" in a blue sea with two boats as well. This model was made in 1812 by prisoners of war at Bishop's Waltham, Hants, and has gun retracting mechanism incorporated. See plate 7.12.

United States Naval Academy, Annapolis, Maryland
The five wood models made by prisoners of war, and shown at this museum, are of 40 gun frigates and 74 gun ships. Because of the British conventions in the method of calculating the strength of armaments in a ship (vide. James' *Naval History*, Introduction), certain firing pieces were not counted, for instance carronades were omitted, consequently a ship classed as a 74 might have as many as 88 guns; this

accounts for the discrepancy in the labels at this museum, and the class of ship to which it belonged. Also I am forced to add that these models are described as British ships when actually, as will be seen by the photographs in the catalogue of the museum, the only thing British about them are the flags; for they are clearly French ships masquerading as British. Comparison of the photographs of models numbered 93 (described as an 86 gun ship) and 95 (called the ALEXANDRIA, British 92 gun ship), with the details of the French characteristics I have enumerated in chapter 7, will make this only too clear; in particular the almost vertical rudder post (see drawing 7.1),

11.1 A carvel-built 74 gun ship from the Liverpool Museum collection. Note that this model is rigged with fidded royal masts set abaft the topgallant masts which is unusual but not necessarily incorrect (cf. 10.1) and as, for example, on the four-masted barque LAWHILL of 1892. *The City of Liverpool Museum*

the comparative absence of sheer, and the curved ends to the light coloured side strakes.

Other museums may have examples of wood ship models made by the prisoners, but the ones I have mentioned above are good representatives of this class of model.

11.2   An 88 gun ship also carrying 6 carronades and 40 swivel guns. It is made of boxwood with a copper bottom and has the remains of a flag which is original and of pre-1801 design. *The Glasgow Museum and Art Gallery*

Chapter 12

The scenic and miniature models
Dockyard scenes
Panoramas
Miniatures

The scenic models were unquestionably made by men with a working and intimate knowledge of shipyards, docks and ports. If there were originally many, only a few of the models have now survived the ravages of time, but these few show in lifelike form scenes in the dockyards and harbours; they illustrate, almost like three-dimensional pictures, the busy scenes when ships returned to port, or were sent there for refitting. A description of one or two of these models will show what I mean.

In the Royal United Service Institution was a boxwood model of a French 74 gun ship, five inches long. It stood on the stocks on a sloping base, bow forward, ready for launching. The hull was supported by shores, and was prevented from sliding down the ways by ropes from the stern, which were belayed to bitts and two capstans on the ground. Around the base was balustrading, and it almost required only the crowds to gather for the ceremony of launching. This model was made by a French prisoner of war at Portsmouth in 1800. It is now in the National Maritime Museum at Greenwich.

Another model in Liverpool Museum shows a frigate only two and a half inches long, in the process of being built. It is supported by shores, and some of the deck fittings are in place. The figurehead and the beakhead rails have already been fitted, but the carriages stand empty, waiting for the guns to be mounted. Though the ship itself is unfinished this in no way detracts from the satisfaction one feels when looking at it. In fact, one can imagine that it is dinner time, that the men have temporarily left the yard for their meals, and that shortly they will be back to carry on with the building of the vessel.

A more elaborate dockyard scene which is worth mentioning is that shown illustrated in the catalogue of the Rogers collection of ship models in the United States Naval Academy at Annapolis, pages 108 and 109, edition 1954; pages 129, 130, 131, edition 1971. The photograph shows a 130 gun French ship on the launching ways. On the ground around the ways are all the boats, guns, masts, anchors, yards and tops ready for rigging the ship after launching. The whole dockyard, which is about fourteen inches square, is enclosed by a white fence with red-painted iron railings and with sentry boxes at the corners.

12.1 and 12.2 Two views of a magnificent scenic model of a 130 gun ship ready for launching and fitting out. All her guns, spars, tops and boats are laid out around her

This model is in the Henry Huddleston Rogers Collection at Annapolis, U.S.A. Compare with plates 12.3 and 12.4. *The U.S. Naval Academy Museum, Annapolis, U.S.A.*

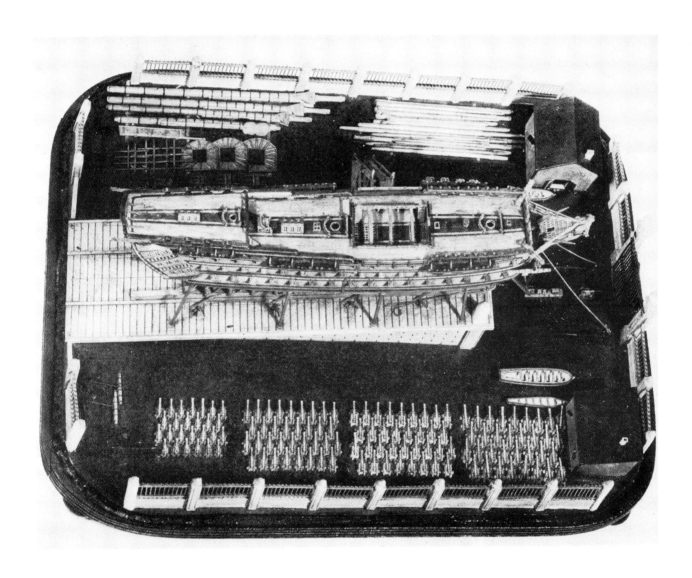

This model dockyard is in the same idiom as the one in Trinity House, which shows an 84 gun ship named the MURAT on a slipway surrounded by the various parts such as guns and masts, waiting ready to be fitted to the ship after she has been launched. There are many points of similarity between these two models, apart from their being basically the same idea; one part in particular, the flight of stairs leading from the ground up to the side of the hull at the waist (for the person who is to perform the launching ceremony?), are so much alike that the oval bone plaque at one end, which says "*Fait par Savagnac à Dartmoor*", could, I feel certain, apply equally well to the model in the Rogers collection at Annapolis.

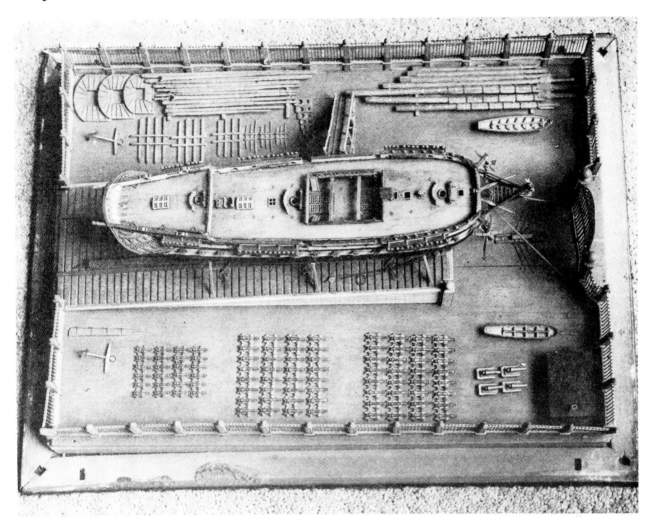

12.3 and 12.4   The 84 gun ship MURAT in the dockyard awaiting her launch.
Made at Dartmoor it bears a striking resemblance to the scene illustrated in plates
12.1 and 12.2. *With the permission of the Elder Brethren, Trinity House, London*

The port and harbour scenes, too, are lively representations of the never ending activity in these places. In the Science Museum is one called "*Vue du Port de Toulon*". These words are fretted in silhouette form, and incorporated in the thin delicate balustrading which surrounds the panorama, and spaced at intervals on the balustrading are eleven figures of angels on pedestals as well as two lions at the corners of the front. The whole is about twelve inches wide and thirteen inches from front to back. The detail shown is of the most diverse kind as will be apparent from the following brief description. At the back of the scene is a coloured straw marquetry picture of the hillside with cottages nestling amongst the tree-covered slopes. In front of this is the promenade where can be seen shops, houses, churches with towers and belfries, and a porticoed walk with tiled roofs. A statue is also to be seen standing on a pedestal.

The harbour itself is surrounded by breakwaters and forts, and divided in two by a central breakwater. Moored on the foreshore, and alongside the jetties, are rowing boats. Various mechanical devices are shown on the breakwaters, such as sheer-legs used in the fitting-out of vessels; and other apparatus for the construction of the ships alongside the central breakwater. A large ship is shown being built on the stocks and is almost ready for its launching, while in the dry dock is a three-deck ship being fitted out. Eight ships in ordinary (that is, out of commission, but laid up in the charge of officers) are anchored at several places. All this covers about half of the baseboard, the other half being devoted to scenes beyond the breakwater.

Outside the harbour is the open sea on which are nine ships, representing three-deckers, two-deckers and frigates, some with sails set and others with sails furled; there are also native craft which are two feluccas and seven tartanes. The largest of the ships is a three-decker only one and a half inches long, but shown with gun ports open and guns run out, and through the open waist can be seen the lower deck. This vessel is towing a dinghy of only three-eighths of an inch long but has the thwarts fitted and the oars lying on them!

The whole model is made of straw and wood. The sea is of straw strips radiating from the centre of the base, and the ships and buildings are of wood. The sails of the ships, where fitted, are of wood shavings and the rigging is of the finest of fine silk and hair. This is a most extraordinary model, giving a vivid picture of the activity and bustle of this important seaport. In fact, so accurate is the model that if comparison is made with the picture "*Vue du vieux port de Toulon*" painted by J. Vernet in 1765, and now in Le Musée de la Marine (5 OA 1), it will be at once apparent that this model is no figment of the imagination or a fictitious harbour scene, but a scenic model made by someone who must have known the port intimately and could possibly have been a resident there or a workman in the dockyard, so alike are they.

A panorama of similar idea in the National Maritime Museum is entitled *"Vue de l'entrée du Port de Marseille. Prise de la Rade"*. This is about twenty-four inches wide and eighteen inches deep, and is shown on a sheet of glass representing the sea, about half an inch above the base. On the glass are water-line ship models, in all

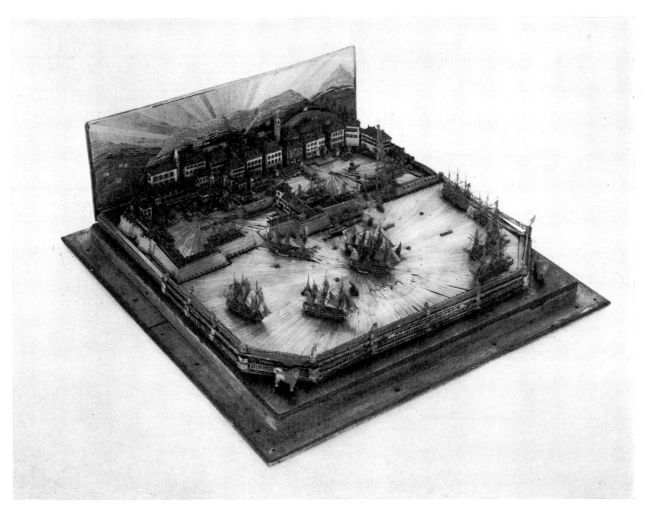

12.5 An amazingly detailed panoramic model of the port of Toulon, only twelve inches wide and made entirely from wood and straw. Eighteen ships plus numerous small craft are shown, some with sails set. A full description is given in the text. *The Science Museum, London*

seventeen ships, of which eleven have sails, and many rowing boats with men in them pulling on the oars. The back of the case has a painted scene of the town, whilst on the glass sea the vessels represented are those of many nations: French, British, Dutch, Sicilian, American, Russian, Greek, an Arab dhow and a paddle-wheeled, high-funnelled, three-masted vessel. Here again the sails are of wood shavings. This model cannot be dated earlier than about 1820 by reason of the round stern of the French vessel, and the paddle-wheel steamer; and so, as is very likely, was presumably made by prisoners who elected to remain in this country.

The miniatures, for want of a better word, of which brief mention has already been made, are in a class entirely by themselves. Liverpool Museum has twenty-two of these models, none of which is above two and a half inches long, the smallest being about one and a half inches long, and yet the detail shown is simply amazing.

This is the Pilkington collection, so called because they were presented to the museum by Lady Mary Pilkington in 1921. The models were discovered in Dublin and brought to England by Lieutenant Tipping on behalf of Sir George Pilkington. Unfortunately they had been sadly neglected and consequently were in need of some repair, which was done by Mr. Andrew Webster Kiddie of Southport in the early 1900's. The restoration has been most beautifully and expertly done by this gentleman who was also a model maker of some repute (an example of his work being the yacht JULLANAR in the Science Museum), and who used for the repair of the rigging, hair from the head of his wife and daughter. For this information I am indebted to his son, Mr. G. A. Kiddie, also of Southport.

The models all follow the same general pattern, as if a school of miniaturists was started to make them, though this must not be taken as meaning that from no other prison came miniatures of exactly similar type, for though all the models are alleged to have been made in the Liverpool prisons, I have found no definite proof that this was so. Furthermore I have already recorded one miniature that was made at Norman Cross, and later in this chapter shall describe one that was made at Gosport. It is possible, indeed most likely, that prisoners were transferred from one prison to another as circumstances rendered it necessary and that the makers of these miniatures carried on with their work in their new situation, and of course at the same time spread, by teaching others, the art of making them. They were obviously not made by one man, for the differences that can be detected

12.6 A miniature model of a 64 gun ship which is made entirely of boxwood, including the sails, rigging, balustrade to the bases and all the fittings. The bases are covered in straw marquetry and the hull of the ship measures two inches long. The model was made at Norman Cross depot and was purchased by Colonel Spencer at Sotheby's, London, in 1936 for £13 and bequeathed by him to Glasgow Art Gallery and Museum from whom permission has been obtained to reproduce this photograph. *Glasgow Art Gallery and Museum*

64
See plate 3.4

65
See plates 6.31 and 12.6

66
See also plate 6.31
67
See plate 3.4

in the quality and style of the work, the class of vessel reproduced, or the stamp which every artist leaves on his work, show that at least four, possibly five, men have made them. Every model stands on a baseboard which may be oval, rhombic, rectangular or hexagonal in shape;[64] frequently this is placed on a second baseboard which is circular, rectangular or hexagonal in shape, and a few are placed on a third baseboard which is hexagonal or circular in shape. These baseboards are surrounded with paper thickness wood or ivory balustrading or picket fencing, and some of the surrounds are festooned in swags.[65] At the corners of the baseboards are placed minute figures or vases on pedestals. These figures, of helmeted warriors armed with a spear or sword, or of angels with palm leaves or wreaths, are no larger than about three-sixteenths or a quarter of an inch in height and yet, kilts, armour, folds to dresses and even features can be distinguished.[66] The floors of the baseboards are decorated with either straw marquetry or wood inlay of a geometrical design.[67]

68
See plate 6.31

The vessels themselves are made of wood, bone or ivory, the sails of wood shavings, and the rigging of fine silk, wood[68] or hair. Amongst them are to be seen representations of 120 gun, 110 gun, and 80 gun ships, a frigate, a polacca, and a clinker-built launch with nine oars to each side, a gun in the bows and a mortar at the stern. Four of the cases have two ships in each of them, one of which shows together an ivory 80 gun ship, one and a half inches long, and an ivory cutter with ten brass guns, three-quarters of an inch long. The other three have each a 100 gun ship with a 10 gun cutter, and there is one case which has in it four ships: a 110 gun ship, a 50 gun frigate, a 10 gun lugger and a 10 gun cutter. Another shows an ivory ship, two inches long, with sails of fish bone, and studding sails set on the starboard side. It is extraordinary the amount of detail that has been included in the ships, in fact one wonders what has been omitted since so much is shown; the decks are laid in planks, the guns are mounted on gun carriages which have wheels, the ladders have hand-rails and steps, and the boats stowed on the decks have thwarts and oars.

Even the cases themselves, averaging about four inches long, three inches high and two inches deep, are interesting. They have four glass sides, the top being of wood; yet underneath the top, the ceiling of the case, so to speak, is also decorated with straw marquetry of geometrical designs, trophies of war, crossed flags or sheaves of flowers and foliage as well. But, unless the case is lifted above eye level, these additions cannot be seen and so could easily be missed.

But the most wonderful of all the miniatures is that in Arlington Court. Made entirely of boxwood, it is an 80 gun two-decker and originates from Gosport. It was inherited from a member of the Golightly family, some of whom lived in Gosport when the French prisoners were confined there during the Napoleonic wars. Below the case is a note in faded ink writing which reads, "Miniature ship made by prisoners of the war of the I Napoleon and bought by Miss Golightly", and is signed Rev. C. P. Golightly.

The ship is about two inches long, and is made of boxwood, with sails of boxwood shavings, and the starboard clew of the main course is drawn up to the bunt. The rigging is made of the silk of the silk-worm, and the shrouds have dead-eyes, lanyards and ratlines. The gun ports, which are about one-fiftieth of an inch square, are open and the port lids are triced up so that the guns can be seen protruding from the ports. A balustrade with a top rail runs round the ship

12.7   A beautifully carved and detailed fully rigged model of an 80 gun ship made entirely of boxwood. It is fully described in the text. *The National Trust Museum, Arlington Court*

merging into the headrails up to the figurehead, which is of a kilted soldier exquisitely carved, and is no larger than about three thirty-seconds of an inch long. The stern is beautifully carved and pierced for latticed windows. A boat about a quarter of an inch long stands on the deck and has thwarts and oars, and another hangs from the stern. There are three masts, topmasts and top-gallant masts, and guns on the gun carriages on deck; in fact no fitting appears to have been left out to make it complete in all details.

But this is not all, for the ship stands on a farm cart, or hay wain, about three inches long and one inch wide. The sides are of delicate filigree leaf pattern, and the floor of the cart is a network of wood. The four wheels are shown with the felloes carved, and the spokes turned, and are made to run on axles. Protruding from the front is the shaft for a pair of horses.

But the model does not finish there, for this stands on a straw marquetry, leaf-patterned, hexagonal base, surrounded by a balustrade that has four angels holding peace offerings of palm leaves, and two vases at the six corners. This in turn stands on another hexagonal base with straw marquetry of leaf design, and has crossed guns at four of the corners. The whole model is in a hexagonal shaped case about four and a half inches in diameter and four inches high. The mind boggles at the work entailed in making this, and leaves one gasping with incredulity that anybody could make such a wonderful model, even under favourable circumstances.

Who made this, and the other miniatures, no one knows with any certainty. It may have been Joseph Julien Piedagnel, who made a minute model of a Revenue cutter, and was known as a fine workman. It may have been Jean Bourg and Emanuel Creuzon,[69] who have already been named as makers of similar if less elaborate models. Whoever they were, they have left us charming and exquisite products of man's handiwork, and if anyone is now mundane enough to ask: What is the use of it all? I shall try to give a satisfactory answer after the next chapter.

69
See plate 3.5

Chapter 13

The scenic models and where they may be seen

Though the panoramic models and miniature models are scarce, they are worth seeing because they are unique. Many ship models have been made since Napoleonic times and will continue to be made, but they are usually to scales of around one-eighth of an inch to a foot, i.e. 1 : 96, and the man who makes miniature models today does not present them in the same way as the prisoner of war models, even though he may work to a similar scale, which was about one-hundredth of an inch to a foot, i.e. 1 : 1200. So in this respect there is nothing to be seen like them, nor has anything been made like them since those days. As for the panoramic models, there are large panoramas in existence, such as the one of the Battle of Trafalgar in the Royal Naval Museum in H.M. Dockyard at Portsmouth but nothing at all of the type I have described in the previous chapter. However, there may be others of which I do not know in private hands; this is undoubtedly a possibility, but as regards the miniature models, it is more than a possibility that there are still some tucked away in somebody's house, for they occasionally show up in an auction sale, where they command high prices if in good condition. Therefore, the following list will be the shortest of the three classes of ship models, but nevertheless very interesting.

Science Museum, London
Panorama, "*Vue du Port de Toulon*". An extremely interesting model and well worth seeing. Described in the previous chapter, and illustrated in plate 12.5.

National Maritime Museum, Greenwich
Panorama, "*Vue de l'entrée du Port de Marseille. Prise de la Rade*". The only other panorama of which I know and described in the

preceding chapter. There is also a two-deck ship about 2 inches long, made of wood with wood sails and rigging, and on a hexagonal base with pillars and two figures at the corners. Also to be seen there is a fanciful model of the VICTORY as Nelson's funeral car. The ship is a full-hull model made of boxwood with brass wales. It is "floating" in a base surrounded by a fretted balustrade, and erected on the deck is a canopy beneath which would be placed the coffin. This model is interesting, as being something different, but to my mind rather grotesque.

Glasgow Art Gallery and Museum, Glasgow, C.3

Three miniatures, all made of boxwood. One case has a three-deck ship 2 inches long and a cutter 1 inch long together. The second case has an 80 gun ship, 3 inches long which has a coppered bottom to the hull. The third model is illustrated on page 143 and is a 64 gun ship 2 inches long, made entirely of boxwood, the bases are covered in straw marquetry, and the pillars of the surrounding balustrades are topped with turned finials or carved figures.

Arlington Court, Barnstaple, Devon.

Only one miniature is to be seen here, and that the finest of any I have ever seen; for this reason I have described it at some length, in the preceding chapter. A model that should be seen if at all possible.

Peterborough Museum, The Priestgate

Bone 74 gun ship, 2 inches long. The fore and main courses are furled, but all the others are set and they are made of fish bone. Straw marquetry base with a diamond pattern. Also in the case, which measures 4 inches long by 2 inches wide by 3 inches high, is a 10 gun corvette which is only $1\frac{1}{2}$ inches long. This model was made at Norman Cross depot and the label attached to it I have quoted on page 22.

Liverpool City Museums, Liverpool

The best collection of miniature models, 29 in all, but 22 cases because some hold more than one model. They are representations of full-rigged ships of from 64 guns to 110 guns, frigates, luggers, cutters, a galley, a gunboat and a frigate on the stocks. They are made of wood, ivory or bone, and have sails of wood, ivory or mother-of-pearl. All are on elaborately decorated bases. The most important collection of miniatures to be seen anywhere, and therefore one that will be worth a visit and repay careful study.

Trinity House, Tower Hill, London

Here can be seen an interesting scenic model of a ship being built on the stocks. All the various fittings are lying on the ground round it, but for a fuller description see the preceding chapter, and plates 12.3 and 12.4

United States Naval Academy, Annapolis, Maryland

A very similar model to the one in Trinity House can be seen here; so alike are they it is quite possible they were both made by the same man. A description can be read in the preceding chapter, and see plates 12.1 and 12.2

Chapter 14

In considering the historical value of the prisoner of war ship models, of whatever materials they may be made, or of whatever type they represent, we are faced with the dilemma of deciding whether they should be classed as authentic representations of actual vessels, or treated as freelance works of art. I think that a general answer to this problem cannot be given one way or another with a clear-cut decision, but that each model has to be judged on its own merits.

Some (admittedly few) appear to be accurate scale models, not necessarily of any particular ship, for that would mean, of course, that they had been constructed with the aid of the draughts of an actual vessel; and how that could have been possible is a mystery to which I am not prepared to offer a definite solution, but there are quite a few models of types of vessels (as opposed to individual named ships) which follow extremely closely the lines to which ships of the period were built, and one or two of which I have noted in the preceding chapters, see plate 10.3. Perhaps the maker, or his fellow prisoner, was a shipwright by profession or even a naval architect, and therefore would know in detail the principles of the design of ships. This is possible, for I have already recorded the statement of a prisoner who employed his time of imprisonment by studying the design and construction of ships, and he could have done this only from a teacher or from books.

Other models bear little or no relationship to any known vessel, but are simply freelance models based on the type they represent. Some are even impossible as real vessels. Some are so exquisitely and fantastically carved that they obviously do not pretend to be scale models, but certainly they merit the description of being beautiful works of art; and as such fetch high prices from collectors whenever they are offered for sale. Some, lastly, are crude, amateurish and ugly, and made by someone entirely lacking the skill of a competent model maker; their only merit being that they are antiques of one hundred and fifty years of age or more.

Reasons for model making

But all are the result of the striving, by men uprooted and torn from their native soil, for some mental stimulus and employment; since frequent reference is made in contemporary accounts of the appalling conditions under which the prisoners lived, and to the thirst for knowledge brought on by the desire to forget their dreary life, their sufferings and their discomforts. For the hours of work and study brought them hours of happiness, and their greatest fear was

14.1 A model which is described as being of H.M.S. BULWARK. It is crudely executed and poorly rigged. The spars and details are much over scale. *The Parker Gallery, London*

Poor quality models

14.2, 14.3 and 14.4   A bone model which is not of the standard usually associated with the subject under discussion, and obviously was not made by a sailor. Witness the crude hull shape and planking and completely flat tuck and stern, the oversize stem and rudder, the way the bowsprit is perched on the stem, the rigging rove through beads, the rudimentary shaping and carving, and the stay over the mast trucks (which never existed). The detail photographs emphasize these points.
R. Creagh-Osborne

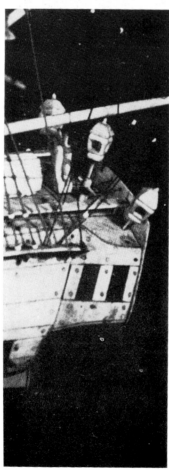

14.5 Though the example of a poor model shown in plate 14.1 was nevertheless probably contemporary the one shown here is almost certainly of more recent construction, probably built between 1900 and 1930, and is thus not a true prisoner of war model. Whoever made this had little idea of the build of a ship. Note the over-large rudder without gudgeons or pintles, the hull shape quite unlike a ship of the period, bad gun ports, silhouette figurehead, poor bowsprit and jibboom, no taper to the masts, meaningless rigging, flat head rails and quarter galleries, and a stay (running from the end of the jibboom over the trucks and down to the stern) which never existed in a fully rigged ship and so cannot be given a name. *Courtesy of Arthur R. Sawers, Chicago, U.S.A.*

that of the "barbaric habit the English had for smashing up pens, inkpots, slates, and burning the paper and books" (as Louis Garneray says) when making organized or routine searches for attempts at escape, and possibly for a less reasonable excuse. To use the modern phrase, it was the result of a form of escapism and for rehabilitation to a future peaceful existence.

In their isolation, too, we have a clue to the tremendous amount of patience displayed, the intricacy of the design, and the superfluity of detail which so characterizes the models. Time was of no account, the future was uncertain, and having once started a model, the maker would go on adding bits and pieces here and there, whether accurate in detail or relevant to the original, if indeed there ever was an original. For it must be admitted that many of the models, though purporting to be of a certain vessel, are quite unlike the prototype. Some bearing the name PRINCE OF WALES, ROYAL SOVEREIGN or VICTORY are so erroneous that neither Calder, Collingwood nor Nelson would have recognized them as the ships they sailed in.

Potential of sales   But as I have suggested, they would be sold to relatives of seamen who served in the ships whose name they bore, and the general outline would be near enough for them. Therefore, they must not be taken too seriously as correct reproductions, even if we exclude the elaborate decoration; nor the names on the models accepted as evidence that the real ship was exactly like the model purports it to have been. For the original draughts of practically all the well-known ships of the period exist, and can be seen in, and copies purchased from, the National Maritime Museum, and if comparison is made between many of the models and the draught, it will be only too clearly evident that the maker knew very little about the actual ship whose name it bears.

However, the makers had obviously served in the foreign ships represented, and would have known them intimately. Their fellow prisoners also would have known of further details. Consequently, what appears to have happened is that the makers have made models of, say, a 100 gun ship, or what was the most popular class of vessel of the day, a 74 gun ship, and though they have built them in the fashion of their own country's ships, they have given them names of their own ships such as the RAYO, a Spanish 100 gun ship, HEROS, a French 74 gun ship, or ACHILLE, another French 74 gun ship; but seeing they were being made primarily for sale to an English customer, what more natural than that they should alter the name to one which was well known to any patriot in this land, such as VICTORY, 100 guns, MARS, 74 guns, or BRITANNIA, 100 guns, and offer it to the gullible purchaser as an accurate model of their son's or husband's ship, or of one that had recently distinguished itself in some naval encounter.

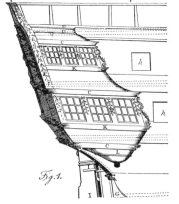

14.6   Quarter gallery of a 74 gun ship taken from Falconer's *Universal Dictionary of the Marine*

Elaborately carved balustrades would not appear in the real ships in the positions shown in many cases; as for instance around the openings in the waist where boats would be swung in and out from the skid beams, nor carved wood panels to simulate hanging drapery be placed alongside the gangways or bulwarks, neither was there so much carved work on the bows or the stern and quarter galleries in the ships of the period. Though the latter were distinctive features of the larger vessels their construction in a model can be quite difficult because of the complication of the angles involved. Their purpose was not purely decorative but to give light to the captain's and officer's cabins in the stern, therefore the windows in the quarter galleries should be in line with the deck and the gun ports as in the contemporary drawing from Falconer (plate 7.1 and plate 14.6), and as in the models of the OCEAN (plate 8.9), the 46 gun frigate (plate 10.3) and the 74 gun ship (plate 11.1). In some models the quarter galleries do not line up in this way but appear to have been made by some other hand away from the model to which they are attached, as in plate 8.6 where the carving does not seem to match up with that on the waist, or in plate 8.5 where the maker's skill has proved inadequate to cope with the problem, the lights being horizontal at the top but getting progressively more out of line towards the bottom. Or in plate 14.7 (which is a very nice model) where the quarter gallery is set too high. In

14.7　A French-built ship carrying 128 guns. Eighteen inches in length overall. Eighteen inches high. A typical example of prisoner of war models being overgunned. It is worth noting the excellent way in which the hull is planked and the regularity of the riveting. The planks are beautifully laid and, what is quite exceptional in a model of this size, they are without joins, being single lengths from stem to stern. The lower masts are fished and woolded. The carved quarter galleries and the figurehead, however, are in marked contrast, being of inferior quality and quite possibly made by a different hand. *The U.S. Naval Academy Museum, Annapolis, U.S.A.*

some cases the windows are glazed and have window bars made of split straw as in the model in plate 7.2. But the general standard of accuracy can be high, and in the main accuracy is sometimes attained. The makers would know the smallest detail in regard to the number and types of guns and the ornamentation which was prevalent in the ships of that period, though it was less prolific than in those of the early eighteenth century, and of which the 80 gun ship, CESAR, in Dover Museum or the model of the NEPTUNE, 98 guns, in Woburn Abbey are fair examples.

Those which have the original rigging intact are more reliable from a rigging point of view; for the work was done by seamen who knew all the details, and many instances can be named where peculiarities of rigging have been proved correct from the evidence of other authorities. But if "restored" by an ignorant person with a meaningless smother of gear, are entirely without value in regard to their authenticity. Yet, conversely, if repaired by an expert, who is sympathetic towards his subject, and is careful and unswerving in replacing any damaged parts exactly as they were, so far as he is able to ascertain from the broken pieces, and does not attempt to "correct" or "improve" anything he might consider wrong, then one must place them on a par with those that have the original rigging.

Yet the makers would not know the exact dimensions and lines of every hull, so, in such respects, the models can be of little historical value, though they need not be too far out of proportion. Broadly speaking, in fact, ship models made by seamen of whatever era or nation, whether sailing ships or powered vessels, are often inaccurate to a certain extent as regards scale detail. This is often due, it must be admitted, to the circumstances under which they are made, and is no reflection on the motive or skill which impels these men to make their models, but is merely characteristic of many of them.

Their motive, more often than not, was one of affection, one might almost say love, for the ship, which may have been the one in which the maker had served. The result naturally varies with the workman, but many of those that have survived display tremendous skill in the use of the inadequate tools and unsuitable materials available, and reflect great credit on the makers. More often than not, no accurate drawings or plans are available to the sailor, so he is forced to construct his model either when he is aboard the ship, or else afterwards from memory. Under the latter circumstance it goes without saying that his recollection of the ship can be false, for memory

14.8   A nicely proportioned 74 gun ship with beautifully laid strakes, the butts being well spaced. Probably not the original rigging but excellently restored. *Courtesy of Christie & Co. Ltd., London*

can play strange tricks on us, as we all know. But as regards the former circumstance, one would have thought that this was the finest way to make a model.

Yet a little reflection will show that this is not so; for instance, the sailor sees the ship from inboard, and he might have little opportunity to see it from a distance. He is too close to his subject, and would rarely see it in its true proportions. To him the mainmast is a tall, tremendous, thick baulk of timber, that towers up till the truck reaches the sky. The bowsprit appears to point upwards at a steeper angle than it actually does. To him the breadth of the deck is small in relation to its length, and in the absence of any means of measuring, he is unable to co-ordinate the measurements of the heights of the masts to the length of the deck. Again, he is unable to assess correctly the shape of the bow and of the stern, nor the shape of the midship section of the hull.

We must, therefore, view with a very critical eye much of the detail that is shown, in many cases with such an abundant and liberal hand, and with some suspicion any very unusual fitting; though it must be admitted, that even these are sometimes authenticated from other sources. But generally speaking, the deck fittings are good, and almost always follow the French or Continental practice of the day, while the rigging is most carefully done usually in the English fashion.

The wood models are usually the more accurate, both in appearance and proportions, and may often be accepted as reasonable representations of the French ships they portray. But in the bone models, the difficulties of working with this material are reflected in the inferior quality of both the proportions and the shapes of the hulls. The decoration tends to become repetitive, and in the worst cases purely imaginary, with little relationship to any known British or French vessel.

Thus, when assessing the historical value of the models, it must be remembered that they were made primarily to while away the interminable hours of captivity, with the secondary object of their being sold. On the other hand, and this seems to me to be quite important, they do fill a gap between about 1793, when war broke out with France, and 1815, when peace returned to Europe. Prior to 1793 our chief source of knowledge of ships, apart from draughts of the designs, comes from the authentic dockyard or Navy Board models, which were made very often before ever a ship was laid down, and sometimes the model is of a ship that never existed, but is of one that it was proposed to build. After 1815 the practice was resumed, but in a much less detailed fashion; for then we find only half-block models being made, other than in exceptional circumstances for especial cases. In fact, the scarcity of good ship models of the succeeding one hundred years is such as to make the task of the researcher into maritime history one of greater difficulty than would otherwise be the case.

Therefore, the prisoner of war ship models do provide us with a link in the evolution of the sailing ship, and moreover incontrovertible evidence of contemporary practice. For they were made by practical seamen, and in this way they add to the store of human knowledge of bygone days.

The cash value of the models

If I am asked, as I have often been, how much a model is worth in hard cash, there is only one answer, which paradoxically is no answer at all—it is worth what you can get for it—and seeing that the prices realized for prisoner of war models at auction of late years have increased beyond one's wildest expectation, any figure I might put on a model today could look ridiculous in a year's time. For instance, the miniature model in Glasgow Museum of a 64 gun three-deck ship made of boxwood, and illustrated in plate 12.6, was bought in 1936 for £13! Such a model if offered today could realize anything between fifty and one hundred times as much! But one thing I do know, and that is what it is that constitutes a good prisoner of war bone ship model, and what to look for in the ideal, but probably unobtainable, model.

70
See plates 2.4 and 8.10

First, the glass or straw marquetry case should be the original one, and though these are to be found they are naturally very rare.[70] The baseboard should be in perfect condition, and whether of bone inlay, wood inlay or straw marquetry really does not matter a lot. As regards the model itself, it should be undamaged and the rigging original. It should be as clean as could be reasonably expected; and can be even after all these years if it has been kept under cover. The proportions of the model should be as near scale accuracy as possible, without being too pernickety in this respect, but allowing for the legitimate inaccuracies to which I have called attention. The carving need not be excessive but what there is should be clear, clean cut, of good design and of artistic merit. The figurehead of whatever character, whether classical, nautical or military bearing, should be of good design and should be part of the stem, so that the drapery or attitude of the figure continues the flow of the rake of the stem. The rails to the head and the whole structure of the bow should flow in sweeping curves. The same applies to the stern and quarter galleries, they should be part of the ship and not just stuck on, the curves of the stern walks should continue into the side galleries and the windows be of adequate dimensions and placed where they would give light to the cabins. The carved decoration of the stern should be artistic and delicate, and fill as far as possible the spaces available. The fittings about the deck should be of scale sizes and the decoration as much or as little as is required to give an interesting appearance. The deck planking should be of scale width or, at least, not be excessively wide and the hull planking, too, should be as near scale size as is reasonable, and each side should be the mirror view of the other. The butt joints of the planks should be staggered and should meet on the lines of the imaginary frames. There should be no stealers, but the strakes should run from bow to stern in a gentle curve. The gun ports should follow the line of the decks and the guns should protrude equal amounts. If possible the gun retracting mechanism, if there is any, should be in working order. The masts should stand at suitable angles when viewed from broadside and be vertical when viewed from aft. The woolding may be black cotton or gold metal, or both alternately, it does not really matter. The tops should be

14.9   No seaman ever made this model. The hull is shaped like a barrel and the stern gallery is stuck on one end. The figurehead protrudes in an unsightly fashion. The rigging is unworkable and the bobstay is attached behind the figurehead. It is included only as showing how bad a model can be. *Author's collection*

horizontal, as also should be the crosstrees and trestle trees. The blocks and dead-eyes should be of scale proportions and the rigging should be of different size rope to correspond with its purpose, whether as anchor cable, shrouds, mainstay or thin running rigging.

This is the ideal, and some I have seen and described in this book do approach it but they are few and far between. But if the ideal is unobtainable there are many which, having been skilfully and carefully restored by an expert with appreciative hands, will command a price far beyond that which the prisoner of war who made it received, and be of a value which with the passing of the years can only increase.

Epilogue

Probably no one is more conscious of the shortcomings of this book than I am, nor of the incompleteness of the picture. I realize there are many gaps in the narrative, many pieces missing from the puzzle, and I do not doubt that the last word has not been said on the subject.

There is much that has been conjectured here, but nothing without a basis of fact. There is nothing that can be said to be pure guesswork, and yet I know from my own experiences, that up and down the country in isolated and obscure places, there are examples of prisoner work which might easily yield further information about this fascinating subject.

A century and a half have passed since these men were imprisoned in this country, and in this time memories have faded, facts have been forgotten and examples have been lost, perished or destroyed for a variety of reasons. Age, decay, neglect and disinterestedness, all have taken their toll and are still so doing.

In this period, too, a multitude of fanciful tales have been woven round the subject, hiding the true facts. Stories of poor, neglected and starving Frenchmen working in dark, dismal dungeons, on materials smuggled into the prisons, and secretly and laboriously carving with penknives and nails the intricate and exquisite ornaments and models I have attempted to describe are too fanciful to be true. The task would be an impossible one. Tales of these fragile and delicate models being let down in baskets by cords from the windows of Liverpool prison, for sale to passers-by in the street, are without foundation as well; though the stories persist in spite of the fact that the prison was surrounded by a high brick wall and that access to the prisoners was fairly unrestricted. And when an article, as recently as a few months ago, in the colour magazine of a reputable daily newspaper states that the models "currently fetching unbelievable prices" were carved by prisoners from "bones in their soup", it shows what rubbish is written about them.

But when stripped of the glamour and fantasy that in the passing decades has arisen around the story, the plain and unvarnished truth that emerges possesses an attractiveness that, if unadorned, certainly is no less remarkable. We can only marvel at the heights to which man's ingenuity, skill and patience can rise in spite of, perhaps because of, adversity.

Tailpiece A prisoner at his work wearing the saffron yellow prison clothes stencilled TO front and back. His light is a wick in mutton fat lying in an oyster shell. From an oil painting by R. M. Coombs.

Appendices

APPENDIX I

COLLECTIONS OF PRISONER-OF-WAR SHIP MODELS

The following list does not pretend, by any means, to be exhaustive. It is merely representative of the places where the models may be seen. From the point of view of quality, the examples in the Science Museum must rank first. Second to them I would place those in the National Maritime Museum. For variety, a journey to Arlington Court will satisfy anyone, for there he will see upwards of fifty specimens of all qualities. At Liverpool is displayed the finest collection of miniatures and at Peterborough, as well as ship models, there is an enormous range of prisoner of war work of all sorts. There are also several well-known business houses which specialize in Marine artefacts and frequently have them on view; nor should be forgotten those internationally known auctioneers who have regular sales of works of art where the occasional prisoner of war model is offered.

London, National Maritime Museum. Greenwich.
London, Science Museum. South Kensington.
London, Victoria and Albert Museum. South Kensington.
London, Trinity House. Tower Hill.
London, Watermen's Hall. 18 St. Mary-at-Hill.
London, Fishmonger's Hall. London Bridge.
Bristol, City Museum. Queen's Road.
Edinburgh, Royal Scottish Museum.
Glasgow, Art Galleries and Museum.
Hastings, Museum. High Street. Old Town.
Lewes, Anne of Cleves' House. Southover.
Liverpool, Museum and Art Gallery.
Dover, Museum. Ladywell.
Arlington, Arlington Court. Barnstaple.
Peebles, Chambers Institute Museum.

Whitby, Museum. Pannett Park.
Stromness, Orkney Natural History Museum.
South Shields, Museum. Ocean Road.
Peterborough, Museum. The Priestgate.
Rochester, Eastgate House Museum. High Street.
Southampton, Wool House Maritime Museum.
Portsmouth, Royal Naval Museum, H.M. Dockyard.
Edinburgh, The Castle.
Worthing, Museum and Art Gallery. Chapel Road.
Southsea, Southsea Castle. Clarence Esplanade.
Oxford, Pitt-Rivers Museum. Parks Road.
Hertford, Hertford House.
Woburn, Woburn Abbey.
Dartmouth, Royal Naval College.
Paris, Le Musée de la Marine. Palais de Chaillot.
Boston, Massachusetts. Museum of Fine Arts.
Annapolis, Maryland. United States Naval Academy Museum.

Apart from the following dealers in prisoner of war ship models, there are many others who offer them for sale, privately or at auction.

The Parker Gallery. Albemarle Street. London.
Christie, Manson & Woods. St. James's. London.
Sotheby & Co. New Bond Street. London.
Wallis & Wallis. Lewes. Sussex.
Bern C. Ritchie & Co., Linden Avenue. Winnetka. Illinois. U.S.A.

APPENDIX II

PLACES WHERE PRISONERS WERE HOUSED

The following list cannot be complete for the very obvious reason that in consequence of the huge number of prisoners, every suitable prison or strong house was used, apart from the private houses where men of higher rank who were on parole were boarded, but it gives an idea of the extent to which it was necessary to go to accommodate them.

Hulks		*Some Names of Vessels*
Chatham	Kent	BRUNSWICK, CANADA, CROWN PRINCE
Gillingham	Kent	SAMPSON
Rochester	Kent	SANDWICH
Portsmouth	Hampshire	SUFFOLK, GUILDFORD, PORTLAND
Portchester River	Hampshire	PROTHEE, CROWN
Gosport	Hampshire	YORK, VENGEANCE
Plymouth	Devon	BIENFAISANT, EUROPE, PRUDENT
Devonport	Devon	CAPTIVITY
Deptford	London	DISCOVERY, LION, DOLPHIN
Woolwich	London	JUSTITIA, CENSOR, WARRIOR

Farms	
Roscrow, near Falmouth	Cornwall
Kergilliack, near Falmouth	Cornwall

Borough Gaols
Savoy	London
Wellclose Square	London

Strong Houses
Wool House, Southampton	Hampshire
Bishop's Waltham	Hampshire
Leek	Staffordshire
Pottery Works, Liverpool	Lancashire
Sissinghurst	Kent
Great Gateway, St. Albans	Hertfordshire

Prisons
Norman Cross, Stilton	Huntingdonshire
Dartmoor	Devon
Plymouth	Devon
Millbay	Devon
Perth	Scotland
Edinburgh	Scotland
Valleyfield	Scotland
Winchester	Hampshire
Portsmouth	Hampshire
Portchester Castle	Hampshire
Forton, near Gosport	Hampshire
Hilsea, near Portsmouth	Hampshire
Bristol	Somerset

Prisons—cont.

Taunton	Somerset
Stapleton	Somerset
Dorchester	Dorset
Leek	Staffordshire
Dover Castle	Kent
Chatham	Kent
Tonbridge	Kent
Liverpool	Lancashire
Manchester	Lancashire
Preston	Lancashire
Lancaster Castle	Lancashire
Lewes Castle	Sussex
Lewes Naval Prison	Sussex
Shrewsbury	Shropshire
Yarmouth	Norfolk
Tynemouth	Northumberland
Penryn	Cornwall
Falmouth	Cornwall
Selkirk	Selkirkshire
Chesterfield	Derbyshire

APPENDIX III

GLOSSARY

These definitions of technical terms, for the benefit of anyone not familiar with them, are taken from Falconer 1769 and Steel 1794.

BILGE. The part of the ship's hull which would rest on the ground if she were heeled over.

BOOMKIN or BUMKIN. A short boom protruding from the bows to extend the lower corners of the foresail.

BUNT. The upper middle part of a square sail.

CAP. A thick block of wood at the masthead, to confine two masts together.

CAT HEADS. Two short beams projecting over the bows from which to suspend the anchor.

CHAIN WALES, pronounced CHANNELS. Broad planks projecting horizontally from the side of the hull on which were situated the dead-eyes for the lower shrouds; see plates 5.13 and 6.23.

CLEW. The ends of the cords of the hammock which, gathered together, suspended it. Also, the lower corner of a square sail.

COUNTER. The part of the ship's hull below the stern gallery.

CROSS JACK, pronounced CROJACK. The lowest yard on the mizenmast. A sail was not normally set on this yard; see plate 6.30.

CROSSTREES. Pieces of timber crossing the trestle trees to support the top.

DAVITS. Pieces of timber extended from the ship on which were hung the boats.

EUPHROE. A long block on the stay extending a complication of small cords called the crows footing from the top, to prevent the topsail from catching under the rim of the top.

GARBOARD. The first strake next to the keel.

GUDGEON. Clamp bolted on the stern of a ship to receive the pintle of the rudder, so turning as a hinge.

HAMMOCK NETTING. Rope netting supported on stanchions at the deck sides, in which were stowed the sailors' hammocks as a safeguard against splinters or small-arms fire.

HANCE. That end of the bulwark where it drops down at the waist.

ORLOP. The lowest deck of a ship, just above the hold.

PINTLE. Small metal bolts fastened to the fore edge of the rudder, with their points downwards, in order to enter the gudgeons.

POOP. The highest and aftmost deck of a ship.

PREVENTER STAY. An additional rope employed to support another.

RATLINES. The small cords, like the rungs of a ladder, to gather the shrouds together.

SCARF. A joint in which the two ends are tapered and let into each other, so that the timber becomes even.

SHEER. The longitudinal curve of a ship's topside.

SHROUDS. The cords from the top of a mast to the ship's side to support the mast. See plate 6.23.

SPANKER. A fore and aft sail set abaft the mizenmast.

STEALER. A short piece of plank let in between two strakes at the bow or stern.

STUDDING SAILS. Light sails extended beyond the principal sails. Colloquially called STUN'SLS.

TAFFRAIL. The curved work at the upper end of a ship's stern, and usually ornamented.

TOMPION. A plug inserted in the muzzle of the gun.

TOP. A platform surrounding the head of the lower masts.

TREENAILS. Cylindrical pins of oak to fasten the plank to the frames.

TRESTLE TREES. Bars fixed horizontally to support the top.

TRUCK. The button at the extreme top of a mast.

WOOLDING. Rope banding passed round the mast to strengthen it.

APPENDIX IV

BIBLIOGRAPHY

T. J. Walker. *The Depot for Prisoners of War at Norman Cross.* Constable. 1915

Basil Thomson. *The Story of Dartmoor.* Heinemann. 1907

Francis Abell. *Prisoners of War in Britain. 1756–1815.* H. Milford. 1914

Benjamin F. Palmer. *Diary of Dartmoor Prison.* Connecticut Acorn Club. 1914

Benjamin Waterhouse. *Journal of a Young Man of Massachusetts. 1816.* New York Magazine of History. 1905

Kenneth Roberts. *The Lively Lady.* Tandem. 1967

Frank Bowen. *From Carrack to Clipper.* Staples. 1948

George Borrow. *Lavengro.* Everyman Library. J. M. Dent. 1906

Herman Melville. *Moby Dick.* Everyman Library. J. M. Dent. 1907

Charles Freeman. *Luton and the Hat Industry.* Corporation of Luton Museum and Art Gallery. 1953

William Sievwright. *Historical Sketch of the Old Depot.* Perth. 1894

Justin Atholl. *The Prison on the Moor.* J. Long Ltd. 1953

Sir William Beveridge. *Prices and Wages in England.* Longmans. 1939

Louis Garneray. *Mes Pontons.* France. 1861

C. Fox Smith. *Ship Models.* Country Life Ltd. 1951

Henry Rogers. *Ship Models at the United States Naval Academy.* America. 1954

W. Branch-Johnson. *The English Prison Hulks.* Christopher Johnson. 1957

Oliver Elton. *Locks, Bolts and Bars.* F. Muller. 1945

Alec Purves. *Flags for Ship Modellers.* Percival Marshall. 1950

Edward Boys. *Narrative of Captivity.* J. F. Dove. 1831

James Choyce. *Log of a Jack Tar.* Fisher Unwin. 1891

Captain O'Brien. *Captivity in France.* V. Lovett Cameron. 1811

Donald de Carle. *Watch and Clock Encyclopedia.* N. A. G. Press. 1950

Clifford W. Ashley. *Book of Knots.* Faber. 1947

Edward Fraser. *The Enemy at Trafalgar.* Hodder and Stoughton. 1906

Dorothy Vinter. *The Old French Prison. Stapleton.* Transactions of the Bristol Archaeological Soc., vol. 75. 1955

Crosby. *Complete Pocket Gazette.* 1818

Commissioner Serles. *Report to the Transport Board.* 1800

Report of the Transport Board to the House of Commons. 1798.

Correspondence with the French Government relative to Prisoners of War. 1801

Chambers's Journal. No. 21. 1854

The Connoisseur. November. 1921

The Banker's Magazine. Vol. 67

Peterborough Advertiser. February and March. 1906

Catalogue of Ship Models at the Science Museum. London. 1952

Kelly. *Cambist of 1811*

Ships and Ship Models. Percival Marshall. 1930–1939

Model Maker, later named *Model Boats.* M.A.P. Ltd. Hemel Hempstead

Marine Models. 1930–1939. Golden House. London

The Mariner's Mirror. Journal of the Society for Nautical Research. National Maritime Museum. Greenwich.

D'Arcy Lever. *The Young Sea Officer's Sheet Anchor.* 1819

David Steel. *Elements and Practice of Rigging and Seamanship.* 1794

William Falconer. *Dictionary of the Marine.* 1769

Gervis Frere-Cook. *The Decorative Arts of the Mariner.* Cassell. 1966

William James. *The Naval History of Great Britain.* 1826